Untied

The Poetry of How Knots Become Strings

by

John Roedel

JOHN ROEDEL

Copyright © 2019 by **John Roedel**

All rights reserved. No part of this publication may be reproduced, distributed or transmitted in any form or by any means, without prior written permission.

John Roedel
 Wyoming /82001
 www.heygodheyjohn.com

Publisher's Note: This is a work of fiction. Names, characters, places, and incidents are a product of the author's imagination. Locales and public names are sometimes used for atmospheric purposes. Any resemblance to actual people, living or dead, or to businesses, companies, events, institutions, or locales is completely coincidental.

Book Layout © 2017 BookDesignTemplates.com

Untied/John Roedel -- 1st ed.
ISBN-13: 978-1702095648

UNTIED

Dedicated to my cousin, Katheryne,

for always having bail money for me.

Maybe

maybe the holes in our hearts

that we are walking around with

are in the exact shape of the

people that we haven't forgiven yet

maybe the scars we accumulate

from this world are just

reminders of the people we gave

up on and then tried to forget

maybe I'll wake up tomorrow and

remember everything that I learned

in heaven before I was sent by a

moonbeam down here to Earth

maybe someday the two of us

will quit looking into the eye

of the devil and asking her to tell

UNTIED

us how much we are both worth

maybe I'll quit drinking red wine after

midnight so I can be brave enough

to go outside to beg a passing angel

for a passionate kiss of peace

maybe we should discount

the drive for perfection and to allow

our souls to know the freedom of

living with wrinkles and a fat crease

maybe I'm hurting inside more

than I have ever been able

to say out loud to you because

I'm afraid that you'll walk out the door

maybe we have all become too good

at hiding all our open wound from

other people because we are certain

that they will give each us one more

maybe the day will come when

empathy will become more important

than winning every single

needless fight that we get in

maybe the day will come when the

ones holding judgment over

us will only count all our graces

instead of how much we sin

maybe I'll embrace the growing

fire inside of me that was started

the moment I put down the noose

I drug with me all around my house

maybe this fire will rise through

UNTIED

me and into this world and

become a blaze that all the

wet blankets won't be able to douse

maybe love isn't just tolerating

somebody for all of them

weaknesses or how they

don't see the world the way we do

maybe love is holding another

in our arms after they fail us and

to sing them to sleep with a

lullaby that they once knew

maybe we are all threads that

can too easily get tangled up

together in a ball of multicolored

twisted fabrics of old string

JOHN ROEDEL

maybe we would all be kinder

once we all discovered

that these knots we tie in each other

cause the worst kind of suffering

maybe maybe maybe

our time here is short

maybe we can treat

every second like a divine gift

maybe we can fight

the dark night as one

maybe together -

the lazy sunrise we can lift

maybe maybe maybe

we scream too much

maybe our growing silence

between us has gotten worse

UNTIED

maybe we can become

northern lights for each other

maybe the two of us

can relight this universe

maybe maybe maybe

I will be gone soon

maybe you will have to

leave this place too

maybe maybe maybe

we should stop being shovels

maybe we should instead

become a fresh jar of glue

maybe maybe maybe

you will give me a

JOHN ROEDEL

taste of your mercy

even if I don't deserve it

maybe then I can squeeze

into the missing piece

of your broken heart

- where only I can fit

maybe maybe maybe

UNTIED

The State of Transition

the only thing to say

when somebody tells

you that you've changed

is:

"Thank you."

over the past couple years

people have told me that they

miss the old me

they miss

the funny me

the less serious me

the safe me

but the thing is,

what they don't know about me

JOHN ROEDEL

is that my favorite places are thresholds

I have about four new beginnings a week

I'll try this and then

I'll try being that

I'll write a poem today

I'll take some photos tomorrow

and I'll tell some jokes on stage next week

and a decade from now I'll be a painting sunflowers

and it will all be the most important thing I've ever done

I'm in a perpetual state of transition

UNTIED

I keep leaving who I was and returning as who I need to be

I don't want to be the same person I was when you last saw me yesterday

too much has happened since then

from what I've heard from the spirits in the trees is that heaven isn't a static place

heaven looks like a thunderhead draping itself over a Rocky Mountain valley

heaven is billowing

heaven is rolling

heaven is churning

heaven is always changing forms

heaven never looks the same from one day to the next

grace is a whirling spectrum of color and heaven has to keep

changing its form in order to keep up with it

heaven changes its camouflage of miracles and magic every morning

and if that's good enough for heaven

then it's good enough for me

there is so much creation taking place around us

so many new opportunities

so many new people

so many galaxies being formed

so much ancient beauty being rediscovered

with all of that going on

how can we not change?

UNTIED

I believe epiphanies aren't meant to drop

they're meant to flood

when somebody accuses you of changing

take it as a compliment and wonder

why they haven't?

don't let your seasons become permanent

let them all pass through you

bloom red

change

bloom grey

change

bloom green

change

bloom rainbows

our souls are made of moving

water

with bits of sunlight in it

we are a glowing ripple

passing through time

heaven is called to reinvent itself daily

as are we

as are we

as are we

UNTIED

Constant Vacancy

you keep telling

me that I'm

empty inside

I'm not,

my love,

there is a

purpose for

my constant

vacancy

I'm leaving

plenty of

room for

hope to

move back in

once it comes

back from holiday

without an empty

heart how can my

my life to become a

wide and flowing river?

without a hollow

chamber there

won't be an empty dance floor

for hope to teach me

how to waltz again

fear wants us to fill our

every nook and cranny

with useless trinkets

I'm emptying everything

inside of my soul

UNTIED

to make sure

that I only have room

for the two of us

and chocolate,

of course,

lots of fucking chocolate

JOHN ROEDEL

Sensitive Ways

the higher the wall

the thicker the vines

the taller the obstacle

-the faster hope climbs

the deeper our divide

the shallower we become

the louder they shout

-the more we grow numb

what we are told to be afraid of

shouldn't be what we truly believe

what we're all told to help slaughter

-will someday become what we all grieve

what does Earth look like from space?

is it a bunch of dots, borders and lines?

UNTIED

or is it swirl of dancing seasons and souls

    - is it a bright blue love note from the divine?

I know evil exists on our floating cosmic marble

I know it has a starving fang-filled drooling mouth

I also know that it's so afraid of our nature for empathy

    -than it hangs a sign on every door that reads "keep out!"

I know the shouting match will continue

I know that debate club will rage on

I wish I had the peace dove to end our trench warfare

    - I wish I was a much smarter John.

there aren't enough bricks to keep us safe

and there aren't enough poems to ease my heart

there aren't enough singing angels left in the trees

    -to stop us all from tearing each other apart

go ahead & make every acre an island

go ahead & mock me and my fucking sensitive ways

go ahead & tell me that I'm part of the problem

    -go ahead draw lines in dirt between us to make everything a maze

I might be wrong

can you admit you might be too?

maybe we should listen more to the songbirds

    -than we do the cable news?

the world will spin on and on and on

time will have its terrible and destined say

UNTIED

the walls built between each of us will someday crumble

    - but I believe that compassion will be our new way

What's Left?

"I'm destroyed," I said while standing amid the smoldering ruins of all that I once thought mattered.

"No, you aren't," God replied to me through the sound of the freezing January wind passing through the pines.

"But everything is gone..." I offered quietly.

"Not everything, my love," God said through the bits of sunlight peeking through the ashen post-snowfall clouds.

"What's left?" I asked.

God spoke through the plops of water coming from the slowly melting icicles:

"Your recovery."

We sat together for the rest of the day.

The wind blew.

The sun peeked.

The ice melted.

UNTIED

But

I'm doing my best to hold it all together

But I'm really not

I tried to memorize how to act brave

But I've mostly forgot

I've been told that my heart is a sponge

But I think mine is more of a fat heavy brick

I'd love to go out with you tonight

But as of right now my mind is all too sick

Life once felt like an open field

But now, it has become a narrow hall

The adventure was once oh so large

But my world is now oh so small

I know I was born to effortlessly take flight

I know I was meant to soar with you all around

I know I was meant to have windblown hair

JOHN ROEDEL

I know I've become addicted to the ground

Am I halfway out of this life?

Or am I halfway in?

Is my life on Earth about to end

Or is a new one about to begin?

The front door can feel like a wall

The doorknob rests heavy in my hand

My mind is a thundering race car

My heart is a big brassy marching band

I ask the terrible foggy fear inside of me

If it will let me go outside for just a single day

But it doesn't want me to leave it ever again

My fear begs for me to stay and stay and stay

The ground beneath me is quivering

The air around me is getting thin

UNTIED

The skin on my bones is crawling

The room is starting to spin

Do I stay inside where it's safe?

Or do I go out there and take another shot?

Do I let my life become a lovely ribbon?

Or do I remain a tightly bound knot?

That's when it always happens:

Eventually I hear a knock on the door

With a rhythm that is rather odd

It's the pounding fist of sacred spirit

It's the rapping knuckles of God

"Come out, dear one,

Come out and feel the light

You are more than this fear you have

You were made to be a kite."

JOHN ROEDEL

Eventually I twist the knob and open the door

The warmth of the new sun spills all over me

Untethered to fear now, I rise into the sky

I become weightless, unanchored and free

My love,

Every day we must choose

To stay inside or go out to chase the day

The secret to living an authentic life

Is to not let fear have our final say

So, meet me out there, my love

And let's float around like brave bright kites

Let's dance in the gale like it's a ballroom

Let's leave our fear behind & join the heights

UNTIED

My Ruby Lover

sitting at the bar

with the thin stem

of a wine glass

cradled between

my fat fingers

I've been waiting

to hear her voice

again

I've been waiting

all day

waiting for the

liquid ruby to rise

up and speak to me

I consume her in slow sips

I empty her six times

I am halfway gone

when she finally shows

up in the dregs and seeds

at the bottom of my glass

she whispers

through her

Cabernet lips

a question that

intoxicates me

UNTIED

more than her tannins

ever did

she asks

"when will you believe in miracles again?"

I press my nose to the

porch of the glass she bathes in

drawn in by the bouquet of her essence

the incense of ambrosia rises

in a magenta fog

making an altar out of the bar top

JOHN ROEDEL

transforming the

whiskey bottles into a cloaked choir

turning my chair into a confessional

and me into a shaking child

"tomorrow," I say

my lips still sweet with her

the glass between my fingers begins to hum

the melody to a song I remember being sung

long before I was born - when I was starlight

my Scarlet Lady of The Vine

smiles with the full-bodied smile

of an angel of earthly comforts

UNTIED

that is blended with equal parts of

debauchery and mercy

and softy offers

"baby, tomorrow is already here"

and suddenly I believe in miracles again

and with that my confession is heard

and the choir begins to chant

and I fall into the glass

surrounded by her

decanted by her

enchanted by her

Right Eye Gone

I lost my right eye

a day before

Easter

I was eight

and it was

Holy Saturday

there was a stick

that was just minding

its own business

being used as

a pretend wand

in the hands of

a twelve-year old

pretend wizard

named David

UNTIED

and I ran straight into it

pupil first

the last thing I

remember seeing

with my right eye

was David's expression

As he was casting a spell

to kill an invisible orc

and then came

the indescribable pain

of my exploding peeper

I passed out

when I woke up

about five minutes later

I was I sitting in

my dad's chair

that he spent

two hours a night

reading cold war

mystery novels in

I knew I must

have been in

bad shape if

they were letting

me sit in that chair

I could only open my

left eye

my right eye was sewn shut

UNTIED

with agony

my dad was talking to

me but I couldn't

quite hear what he was saying

the only thing I could focus on

was the sound of my mom

crying behind him

"Open your eyes. Let me look,"

my dad said with hands on my face

I remember his fingers were covered in soil

he must have been gardening

when he got the news that I

had been struck some dark magic

I tried to open my eyes.

JOHN ROEDEL

I couldn't

there was a hungry monster

that moved in under my eyelid

devouring my sight

with a bit of force

my dad helped me pry

my eye open for a fat second

and I watched with my

left eye how his face

turned as grey as

pair of Deacon's pants

"shit..." he said

the light poured into my

right eye like lava

UNTIED

my right eye became fire

and I passed out again

the next thing I remember

I was laying in the back

of my parent's white Zephyr

as they raced me to the hospital

fresh smell of pesticide

my dad had, in fact,

been gardening

poor dad,

one minute he was planting carrots at his

garden downtown

the next he was watching his son

through his rearview mirror

convulse in the back of his car

thus, the life of a parent

from turnips to tragedy

in a heartbeat

my head in my mom's lap

her hands on my forehead

shaking

my mom loved me

but she was never really that physically affectionate

with me

so, the feel of her hands on my head

was like a comet

rare

comforting

celestial

UNTIED

my nose started bleeding

and

I passed out again

I woke up a day later

with an eye patch

the size of Panama

it was Easter

but there would be no resurrection

for my sight

the tomb of my vision still had a stone in front of it

a man in a white

coat came in with

a brown clipboard

and told me even though

I had endured a

six-hour surgery

that my right eye was

destroyed

"Like The Death Star?" I asked

"I don't know what that is," the doctor said

I hated him for that answer

how could an expert

of science and medicine

not know what The Death Star is?

it was in that

exact moment that

I learned to never

trust a person who

was big on clipboards

but little on pop culture

UNTIED

since that day

before Easter,

when I was eight,

when I lost my right eye,

the only thing

I can see are the

things that are

on my left

the things that are on the left of me

and the people who have left me

and what little time that I have left

38 years later,

I am left with

grey hair

and parents who have left me

and a right eye that I am left with

that aches every time it rains

I was left with

the memories

of that big stick

and of David's face

and that red chair with my dad

and that car ride with my mom

and that doctor

and everything that came after

all the good times

and all the bad

but here is the shit of it all

my memories are starting to drift

away

UNTIED

it's all becoming a blur

the details of my past are starting to swirl

and fade and mist and morph

I'm losing my memories

which is terrifying for a guy who has spent

most of his life squinting backwards

for myself, the man with one eye,

the present has always been

my blind spot

but now so is the past

I haven't been able to see what's right in front of me

and now I am having a hard time seeing what's left

The Masterclass

someday

autism will

teach you

that life is

meant to be

viewed through a

Kaleidoscope

in the swirling

colors of people

living with autism

you will find a

pattern of tones

that you will be tempted

to call chaotic

and wild

- but they aren't

UNTIED

the colors of autism

are the tumbling

and flowing patterns of a

life lived without fear

colors without

borders

and patterns

without limits

are what masterpieces

are made of

with your eyes pressed

to the kaleidoscope of autism

you will find yourself

overcome by the

unfolding colors of hope

and unrelenting life

the lionhearted red of courage to overcome our fears

and the soft velvet blue of empathy to live with open hands and not clenched fists

and the clinging late autumn orange of perseverance to not surrender to the dark night

and the yellow sunrise of mercy to treat all life with dignity

and the spring green of emerging life under a blanket of quiet snow

and the Lenten purple of redemption despite our suffering

are just a few of the swirling

colors of autism's

kaleidoscope

if you visit a church

at the exact right time

when the sun is splashing

through a piece of

UNTIED

stained glass you will

know what I'm talking about

colors

and light

don't care

much

for borders

or for order

colors strain

through painted glass to

join the dance and

the swirl

and the mix

of hope and love

and red and blue

and orange and yellow

and green of purple

JOHN ROEDEL

and life and courage

on the stone floor and

empty pews and

on the painted over

walls of our

memory

all creation is art

all life deserves dignity

all colors are designed

foe bleeding into each other

uniformity is a myth

that we let become a

mirror that we use

to put our makeup on

with

when you fix

UNTIED

your gaze inside the

lens of a kaleidoscope heart

nothing is typical or ordinary

when you stare into

the eyes of a person who

is living with autism you

will be wrapped up

in a rainbow of colors

that you never thought

existed before

all the colors

bleed into each other

until what makes

them different is

what makes them

exactly beautiful

just like us

just like us

just like us all

UNTIED

Scar Play

show me

your beautiful scars,

my love,

do not disguise

them

for they are your jewels

there is nothing

sexier than

the tiger lily that

has survived the

long winter

JOHN ROEDEL

show me

where the weight

of the season

stripped you

of your bark

show me

where the axe

fell to

split you

show me

the wound

that they said

UNTIED

would be the

end of you

      - but wasn't

show me

the place

where you

rose like

valley floodwaters

your scars

are not blemishes

they are the

bright pastel colored

feathers from

your wild peacock soul

show me,

my love,

where the bastards

came to destroy you

- but failed

because your roots

run deeper than

the eye of the mantle

their shovels broke

UNTIED

before you did

and now you are

eternal

show me

the bloom

of your injured

perfection

show me

how you

turned your

aching scars into

sweet seductions

JOHN ROEDEL

and I'll show

a summer without

end

UNTIED

Dull Bright Dull Bright Bright Bright

When I was a child I

would often go night fishing

with my dad during

the summer to escape

the noiselessness and heat...

our stuffy house

We would stand in the

same river and

silently say all the same

things that a father

and son are afraid to speak

to each other on land

we spoke our

truth to each

with antique rods

and often-tangled reels

we confessed

our sins to each other

with wiggling worms

flayed out on sharp hooks

we wordlessly

forgave each other

among the moving water

and hungry trout

UNTIED

most of the time I would

go out into the river barefoot

feeling the great

flow pass around

my hairless legs like

it was the holy spirit

moving in slow motion

my toes digging into the

dark mud

my heels pressed against

a couple small smooth

river rocks that time

had been polishing

for a couple thousand years

inevitably once I would

become bored with trying

to catch fish that were always

smarter than me I would turn my

attention to the river rocks

I loved being among the

red of quarter-sized river rocks

they were so uniform

so glassy

UNTIED

and when I would hold

one of them in my hand

it felt like it belonged there

like it was already a part of

my memory

like the we were meant

to find each other

I used to love going night fishing

with my dad

I remember a perfect night

on the river with my dad

JOHN ROEDEL

when I was a new teenager

bright stars

biting mouths

gentle water

toes in mud

surrounded by my friends,

the river rocks

the only thing I could hear

were the whizzes and the following

whirls of our lines casting in and

out into the water

UNTIED

that's when I first saw it

a faint blinking light in the

crowded starfield

of our open

Wyoming night sky

the light stood out

to me because it was

the strangest hue

of green I had ever seen

in the heavens

it had a lime green

tinge to it with

that would flicker

between being

dull and bright

I asked my dad

about the light

but told me that

he didn't see it

I didn't blame him

since it was so very

hard to see

UNTIED

but I became fixated on it

and the bizarre way that it

seemed to increase and

decrease in intensity

it flickered

dull

dull

dull

bright

dull dull

dull

when we left the river that night

JOHN ROEDEL

I forgot all about the light

until

A couple years later

when I was a hardened teenage

my dad took me out

on a very clear night

for what would end up

being the last time we ever

went fishing together

had I known that

I would have brought

a tape recorder

UNTIED

So, I could have

Recorded the sounds

of my father's reflective sighs

and the way the river

babbled and how our

fishing lines tickled

the surface of the water

had I known that this was going

to be our last time fishing

I would have brought

a book of prayers or poems

that we could have read

to each other

had I known that this

would be our final fishing trip

I would have brought

a jar to take some

of the water home

with me

on our last night of night fishing

I saw the green light in the sky

for the second time

it was so much brighter than it

was the last time I saw it

it wasn't a faint flicker anymore

UNTIED

it was a thick lime green bulb

pulsing in some sort

of mysterious rhythm

like a code I couldn't break

bright

dull

dull

bright

bright

bright

dull

I pointed it out to my dad

once again

"There," I said standing behind him as the

water passed around both of us like we were

reeds who had been there for a century

"Look, dad. There is that light I saw a few years ago.

Do you see it now? It's really bright tonight.

What is it?"

my Dad took a sip out of his

can of warm beer and squinted out

into the heavens

UNTIED

"Nope. Sure don't see a light," he responded quietly and went back

to hoisting his line out into the river for a rainbow-backed

fish that he could grill up tomorrow night

I became angry at him for a reason

I couldn't quite place at the time

I turned my finger into a blade

and pointed it straight out the green light in the sky

The light in response sent back another message

bright

dull

dull

bright

bright

bright

bright

dull

"What do you mean you don't see it?" I asked. "It's right there. Right there!"

My father shot me a look of confusion

"Look again!" I said sharply.

"Quiet, you'll scare the fish." he said.

UNTIED

bright

dull

dull

bright

I became frightened

How could he not see it?

Fuck the fish

I wanted him to see the world through my eyes

How could he discount it so quickly?

so typical of our relationship

what in the hell was the green light in the first place?

what if it was a comet that would come to kill us all?

what if it was a UFO that probed first and asked questions later?

what if it was a figment of my imagination?

any answer I came up with scared me

so, I decided to ignore it and went

back to fishing and learning

how to be silent and not

scare fish

while the green light

pulsed above me

bright

dull

dull

UNTIED

dull

bright

we drove home in silence

and packed away our

fishing equipment for the

final time

From that moment on, every time I would look into the night sky. I would see the green light. And every time it would get brighter and brighter - seemingly closer and closer.

nobody ever saw it but me

eventually I stopped asking people

about it because it made me sound like

I had lost my fucking mind

maybe I had

Its blinking message was only up for my interpretation.

bright

dull

bright

bright

dull

dull

bright

Most of the time I would forget about the light during the daytime. I would go about my errands, work and chores without ever giving it a thought....

UNTIED

but then the sun would go down

and the green light would return

it always returned

the green light would

always be adorned

in the exact same

spot every night

always growing closer

always becoming harder to ignore

on the summer afternoon

when my dad died I

started seeing the

green light during the daytime

somehow it stood against the

brilliant wash of the sun

five minutes earlier I had

just gotten off the phone with

my dad's nurse telling me

that his last fistfight with cancer

was beginning

I told her I would head right over

she said "Hurry."

UNTIED

that's when I saw the green light

in the daytime

it cut through the thick July sky

this time the light wouldn't pulse

from dull to bright

it was just bright

bright

bright

bright bright bright

I stopped at a stop sign

on Moore Avenue

and stared up through my

cracked windshield at the

green light that hung

in the blue canvas

like some sort of cosmic

Christmas ornament

I was exhausted

I was terrified

I was losing my sanity

bright

bright

bright

UNTIED

bright

bright bright bright bright

I was so fucking tired

nobody tells you that

saying goodbye

to a parent carves us

up like a picnic honeydew

watching my dad

fade away

had reduced me

down to the last

fragments of my

candlewick

I was broken

bright

bright

there would be no

more fishing with

my dad

bright

bright

bright

UNTIED

there would be no

more silent reconciliation

together among the willows

and the trout

"Leave me alone!" I screamed up at the light

"Leave me the fuck alone!"

I slammed my hand on

the steering wheel

bright

bright

I yelped

and I yammered

until the car behind

me honked for

me to take my mental

breakdown to the

nearest parking spot

I kept driving to the hospital

under the watchful eye

of the green light

bright

bright

bright

UNTIED

something inside

of me told

me that I had

to get there quick

I put my car on the third

floor of the parking lot and ran through

the hospital doors and hallways like

I was late for a flight

turns out I was

by the time I reached

my dad's room

he was gone

he

was

all

gone

the room was quiet

his body was still

I closed my eyes

and felt the moment

drape over me like a cloak

I could feel the water

move around me

UNTIED

I could feel my toes

dig into the mud

I could hear the lines

we cast splashing against

the film of river water

I could hear the babble

I couldn't speak

I didn't want to scare the fish

that day was the last time

I ever saw the green light

in the sky

just like my dad

it vanished

just like my dad

it fell from the sky

until last year

my feet were in the soft white sand

of the tide in South Carolina

my toes were digging in

the sun was setting on the endless horizon

the gulls were barking

the water would roll in around me and then roll out

the blue in the sky was bleeding into and orange that would soon bleed into a dark

UNTIED

I couldn't move

I couldn't speak

I knew what was coming

as the rolled out over

the edge of the world

I saw the faintest of green lights appear

the water moved stirred around me

high tide was coming in

I could hear my dad throwing his fishing line

I could hear him reeling his line back in

I could feel the sacred silence between us return

what was this light? Why Was it back?

my mind spun

is it a memory?

is it time?

is it an angel of change and transition?

or is the light different for all of us?

maybe my dad had seen the green light and didn't want to define it for me

maybe my dad was just as confused as I was about the mysteries of this life

UNTIED

maybe my dad wanted me to discover what the light was for myself?

maybe the point of being a parent is to let our children figure things out on our own?

bright

bright

dull

bright

dull dull dull

dull dull

bright

a small shell

washed up against

my bare feet

I reached down and grabbed it

it felt like one of the river rocks

from the river my dad and I used

to fish in

so smooth

so timeless

I closed it around my fingers

and just like those river rocks

from years ago, it felt like it belonged

in my grasp

UNTIED

it felt like home

it felt like we were supposed to find each other

the green light grew in the now dark sky

bright

bright

bright

I felt a hand on my shoulder.

It was my oldest son who towered

over my small body

"Do you see that weird green light out there?" he asked with his right hand outstretched over me pointing at the green light in the night sky.

the water rose around us

I put my hand up on my shoulder and grabbed his.

"What light?" I asked with tears pouring down my face that was now covered in the softest of green hues.

I could feel the porcelain

shell vibrate in my fist like an old pager.

Yes. Maybe we were all supposed to find each other.

maybe the green light was just a

reminder of how quickly time passes around us

like a river in Wyoming

like a tide in South Carolina

UNTIED

bright

bright

bright

or maybe it's just the light that comes whenever God records

some of our most beautiful memories

brightbrightbrightbrigh

JOHN ROEDEL

Speaking in Velvet Tongues

my love,

remember before you release

your words like Olympic ceremony

doves to make sure that you

cover them in perfumed oils

while they rest on your tongue

soak your words in sacred softness

so, they aren't tempted to

turn into bullets

treat your words

like divine threads

that sew us together

UNTIED

and not spears

meant for

trench warfare

the bitter words

that you allow to

die in your mouth

are the sorts of

coins that

the new world will

use as currency

Little Red Star

as the universe cooled

from its fire birth

the baby stars were chattering

about the adventure ahead of them

a little red star

had one question for God though

"What happens when our

light burns out?"

God turned a nebula

into a megaphone and said

UNTIED

"Oh, my sweet one,

that won't happen for

a very long time"

"but what will happen

to us when it does

go out?" the little red star pressed

"You go Supernova,"

God replied

"What's that?" another baby star asked.

"You'll become 100 million times brighter

and then explode."

the stars grew silent

and started quivering

"Fear not, my lovely ones," God said

from the back of a streaking comet

"Why shouldn't we be afraid?" a brave little yellow star

asked from the middle of the Milky May

"We don't want to die!"

God kissed the little yellow star on the forehead and said

UNTIED

"Oh, my love, all will be well,

light never dies...light always survives.

It just changes form. Light is always in the

process of becoming something else."

the yellow star smiled

and light poured out of her eyes

"I can't wait to see what I become,"

the yellow star said

"Neither can I, little star," God replied

while looking up at her burning light from a café in Paris

Performance

I don't know my character arc

but I know that I am meant

to discover every inch of this stage

we share

I don't remember my blocking

or when to enter

or to exit

but I remember how to stand next to you

despite having legs

that are shaking underneath my pleated pants

I can act brave

I can act like I know what I'm doing

I can act like the skin on my back isn't trying to crawl off

I can act like I deserve you

UNTIED

the only thing I can't do

is to act like my pulse hasn't

somehow matched its rhythm to yours

every time I hear your song

I didn't memorize my lines

but I still know what to say to you

when you place your hand on my face under

the spotlight

"My love,

this doesn't make any sense,

I know it doesn't

   -but I love how you turned

my heart into a flute."

JOHN ROEDEL

I don't know if there is anyone watching

in the audience

and frankly I don't care,

you are my audience of one

I perform only for you

contorting myself to fit your narrative

I improv my way into your future

laying vulnerable in your green room

eating the grapes of your poetry

while you whisper to me the plot

of our next act

the show is starting

UNTIED

the curtains are rising

the lights are crackling

I may have thrown out my script

yet, I know that the lines that

I need to feed you will find their

way out of my mouth

because I have rehearsed for this moment

ever

since the day I auditioned for you

three million performances ago

JOHN ROEDEL

These Little Beautiful Things

I used to

be so careful

about who I showed

all of the little beautiful

things that I could create

I was afraid that

people would

break them and

then these treasures

of mine wouldn't

be beautiful any more

so, I dug a hole

and buried my lovelies

in a grave where all

UNTIED

unknown art goes to

hide from the world

then when I was 40

the moon showed up

at my bedroom window with

a bottle of vodka

and a song

as the moon poured

me a short glass

she sang a tall proverb

"Quit planting

all of your treasures

that you have created

in the dirt."

I replied

"But I'm afraid that

somebody will break them."

"My love," the moon sang

"That's impossible. Everything

you have ever created is already broken.

"Why are they broken?" I asked.

"Because you are broken."

The moon felt my sadness and it rested her head on my shoulder

"What's wrong, dear one?" she sang

UNTIED

"I just want to make beautiful things,"

I said looking straight into growing midnight.

"You will," the moon hummed.

"But I'm broken..."

"Yes, you are - and it's with that brokenness that

you will make something that will reflect light and be so very beautiful."

I drank down her

spirit and her words

in one gulp

"Are you sure?" I asked.

My darling Moon kissed

my cheek and sang a secret

that I had long forgotten:

"Of course, love. If anybody knows about how to take their brokenness and turn it into a reflection of

a beautiful light it is me."

We sat in silence,

holding each other

for an hour until

the orange clouds came from

the lip of the mountains to usher

her back to the beyond

&

that is exactly the moment

when I stopped

being so afraid.

Saltwater Goodbyes

I could tell that this goodbye was different by the way your lips turned to sand after I kissed you goodbye in the car.

"Excuse me," you said with the hint of saltwater on your breath. "I don't know what's happening to me."

I did but I didn't say anything. I just brushed back the dripping seaweed that was covering your eyes and placed one last kiss on your smooth forehead.

You were leaving

Forever

and I was going

be forced to stay

for even longer

the tide had come for you

and I was to remain

sitting by the shore

like a haunted lighthouse

you opened the car door

and the water we were sitting in

poured out into the

pavement of the airport

drop-off zone

the flood created a wide stream

that went

straight to the gate where your plane

was waiting for you

you turned to me

one last time

UNTIED

your eyes

had become seashells

that played the echo

of all of the times I used

to make you laugh

I placed my hand

on the fluorescent

plankton that was

covering your arms

I was crying

and shaking

as you

became surrounded by

a thousand pink seahorses

you couldn't speak

but somehow, I could hear the psalm

you wanted to offer me

ring in my head like a crying gull

"love is an ocean

and I am its song

love is the great deep

and I'm being called

back home."

with that you melted into

the riptide

and joined the other

sirens of the endless

UNTIED

blue mystery

I parked a mile away

and watched as your

plane rose straight into the air

and witnessed it become a pod of dolphins

that you rode right into the

glowing horizon

you were right,

love is an ocean

and you are its song

and for the first time

how I wished that

I hadn't let myself

become an island

JOHN ROEDEL

They're Coming

hurry, my love,

we are running

out of time to say

all the things that

we need to offer

to each other before

they send the crows

to come for our voices

before the coming

great silence

let's sit

in an empty tub together

and let our words pour out

like bathwater

UNTIED

let's wash each other

in spoken mercies until we hear

the heavy knock on the door

let's soak in the rinse of

our forgiveness until

such tender things are

made illegal by pinstriped

cowards

my love,

before we are made to be quiet

can I tell you a secret?

my heart is just a pile

of tiled letters

and every letter is u

does that make any sense?

whenever I try and write

a poem about sunflowers

that I only can scribble a

u over and over

whenever I sing about the peace that

I find in a moving river

the only lyric I could remember was "u"

whenever I became speechless

and didn't know what to say

the only letter resting on my tongue was u

please, my love, please

don't answer the pounding

UNTIED

door just yet

lay in the water of our

unspoken words

pour them over my head

wash me in your whispers

before it's too late

they are about to break the door down

they are almost here

I will not be made to whisper your name

I will not be made to be silent

love is love

and my heart is a jumble of letters

and every single one is u

I will not be made to be silent

I will not be made to be silent

JOHN ROEDEL

Pulling Strings

love is a piece of endless

yarn that each of us agree to

hold on to an end of

gently between our fingers

so that when we get separated

from one another

by the illusion of death

we can tug on it

ever so softly

to send each other messages

back and forth through the slack

UNTIED

as if to say:

"I'm still here.

"We are endless."

I can't wait to see you again."

the connections we make

here on Earth are the most

consecrated of threads

they are unbreakable blessings

that transform the space

that exists between the people

we love into a field of divine strings

pulling on each other

in a choreographed

symphony of moving

tufts of affection

in a spider silk

of stretching

heartfelt vows

in a quid pro quo of

tender exchanges

my string pulling

often sends this message:

"my, love, nothing will

UNTIED

ever come between us

nothing

let us be two kites

forever entangled

in mid air

I am not bound

to the soil but to

your souls

we are tethered

together

like dancing angels

above the tree lines

hold my string

and I'll hold yours

and there will

nothing

that can ever

keep us apart"

love is a string

held between two

people

UNTIED

that holds

them together

it's all such a miracle

I'll never let go of my end

when the night comes tonight

I'll draw on our shared string as if to say

"Goodnight, my love."

and I'll hold my breath until I

feel you pull pack on it

as if to say

"Our love is eternal."

Streetlights

I'm standing under streetlights

just outside your red door

I'm asking God to give me

everything I've searched for

the love of a good woman

a kid or maybe four

a world where debts are butterflies

a world where peace outlives war

my prayers are mostly promises

that I know I'll never keep

I offer to become a true believer

if I'm allowed to finally sleep

I've been awake for days

UNTIED

listening to the murder of crows

who tell me to cut into my skin

and to wrap my neck with a hose

I wish that sleep would take me

and I could find some true rest

I wish that my love would return to me

and lay her hair across my chest

instead I'm standing under streetlights

begging God to intervene

to turn back time and help me find

a way to be made clean

the cold night air is resting

deep inside my lungs

when the wave of unexpected mercy

comes and comes and comes

my fingers start to tingle

my eyes begin to glow

and my faith in the unseen

begins to grow and grow and grow

if this is my conversion

I pray for quick relief

because my doubts are heavier to carry

than the weight of new belief

when you see me under streetlights

just outside your place

please do not come and wake me

for I'll be dreaming in warm grace

UNTIED

Up Up Up

I saw a red balloon rising

that had once tied to a small hand

floating up like a buttercup

straight to the promised land

I lifted too right up out of my socks

to chase a fat racing cloud

and as I reached the gates to life

I heard my name called out loud

"John, why are you way up here," a cirrus asked
through the crystals in her lips

I told her that I was abandoning gravity

to avoid the coming apocalypse

JOHN ROEDEL

The cloud gladly let me pass

after we shared a glass of rain

that turned me into a wingless dove

and left me with no shame

as I danced into the stratosphere

I came across a rising prayer

that long ago had been offered

by a little girl with dirty blonde hair

she asked God for a pure heart

and a love that would be true

but her prayer got stuck up in the sky

and for years never could breakthrough

UNTIED

so, I took her psalm that had got lost

and wrapped it around my wrist

I promised that I would go find her

and come to know her kiss

I felt the pull of Earth's long reach;

its desire for me too great-

I fell back down through the blue

my thoughts of her had become a weight

I landed safely upon her lawn

and I knocked on her front door

the dirty blonde-haired girl opened it

and my words began to pour

"I found this prayer that you once sent

lost up in the great wide blue.

I was wondering, if you don't mind

could I become that man for you?"

she paused and looked me over

seeing the clouds that I did wear

the dirty blonde girl took my hand

and together we both became the air

we left your world - we shot right up

right passed the old North Star

and if you look real closely into the deep

you'll find us where we now are

UNTIED

It'll Be Sublime

this blurring line

between us and

the coming divine

is so very fine

and so is the wine

and yes, you can have mine

and in your arms, I'll align

and to your lips, I'll consign

and you'll be my life

it'll be sublime

it'll be sublime

it'll be sublime

if we recline

under the trees that we climbed

I'll make a shrine

out of acorns and pines

that will stop time

and then I'll place gemstones

on your bare spine

so you'll become a sign

of a grace that shines

it'll be sublime

it'll be sublime

it'll be sublime

while we dine

on smoke, blankets and thyme

don't listen to the swine

let them opine

let them whine

UNTIED

pay them no mind

our love isn't a crime

they won't define

or malign

the way our hearts

have intertwined

like two ancient vines

that complete each other's rhymes

it'll be sublime

it'll be sublime

it'll be sublime

in your eyes I'm confined

and now I'm blind

to only see the word through your mind

because our love was designed

to teach me how to be kind

and to always remind

that joy is meant to be mined

and chewed down to the rind

until our souls are primed

until we leave our sins behind

until between us we find

an unbroken tie that binds

it'll be sublime

it'll be sublime

it'll be sublime

when I'm down to my last dime

when I'm in the quick of my decline

UNTIED

when my bones begin to grind

when my diagnosis isn't benign

when I hear the funeral bells chime

when my death comes at nine

and I'll still be your boy

who gave you his wine

and you'll still be mine

the girl with gemstones on her spine

until the end of time

it'll be sublime

it'll be sublime

it'll be sublime

Invitation

the quieter the morning,

the louder my heart

the more brilliant the light,

the more I fall apart

the unmoving pines

the slow halted breeze

my weak trembling hands

my poor shaking knees

the deep blue sky

the singing robins

my whispered sins

to a God that pardons

UNTIED

the outside roaring splendor

and my invisible aching cysts

have made a truce

and now peacefully coexist

the day is inviting me

with its sly silent smile

to rise and forget

my old scars for a while

to join the full blue

the yellow and the green

to lay down in the river

to be gently washed clean

JOHN ROEDEL

I'll stand when I can

I'll open all the doors

I'll wave to the heavens

I'll let the light pour

I'll hear grace calling

I'll stop trying to hide

I'll fall into the beauty

I'll quit living on the inside

good morning to my big fat yellow sun

good morning to all of my pink flowers, too

good morning to my healing broken red heart

good morning to my daybreak life made anew

Talking with Trees

My wife told me last weekend that we should go on a hike.

"Are you trying to become a young widow?" I asked honestly. I have long suspected that my wife was looking for accidental ways for me to die so she could marry somebody closer to her station.

Jenni know that mixing me with the great outdoors is never a good idea. I always attract wildlife to make an appearance. Sometimes it's snakes. Sometimes it's porcupines. Sometimes it's The Blair Witch. We can never just "go on a hike" - something crazy always seems to happen.

I'm not sure what causes Mother Nature to lose her shit whenever I pay her a visit - I think my fear of her is what turns her on. We have an unhealthy relationship of emotional bondage and torture. Our interactions are like some poorly written fanfiction called "Fifty Shades of Green"

Early on during our *hike I came across a downed tree in the middle of a dense patch of other trees that looked down upon their dead comrade like they were saying goodbye to it at an old-fashioned Irish Wake.

(* *a hike with me is defined as a walk any further than typical distance between the exit of a Target to my car where I complain every 1.4 seconds about being forced to endure light that isn't fluorescent.*)

I sat down by the tree and my mind began to wonder. My wife noticed the look in my eyes and decided that she would go on without me for a bit while I sat there transfixed by a single dead tree. Jenni has seen this expression on my face before and it's not her favorite. It's a look on my kisser that screams "Emo John has taken over. Please start playing some Peter Gabriel music right away and bring him some super expensive coffee to slurp on while he muddles through his feelings."

"I'll be back in a bit," she said. "I'm just going to press on a little further."

UNTIED

"I'll probably be dead by the time you return," I replied.

"Scratch out your last wishes on your skin before you do," she said as she disappeared down the trail.

Great. This is exactly how every horror movie ever starts. The real shit of it all is that I never even got to have sex in the woods before some undead axe murderer will have shown up to slap chop me into pudding.

I couldn't stop staring at the dead tree.

The discussions over whether a tree that falls in an empty forest makes a sound have never been that interesting to me. I don't care if this tree made any last noises as it fell. I just wanted to know why it fell. I want to know if it knew the name of the last bird that sat on one of its branches before it collapsed. I want to know if the tree was obsessed with its own mortality the way that I am with mine. I want to know if it was afraid when it felt itself starting to tip over. I want to know the last thing it thought of before it became prone on the floor of the woods. I want to know how the tree felt whenever a child climbed it. I want to know if it had any kind of a relationship with the local squirrels - were they friends or were they enemies? I bet they were frenemies.

I wanted to know when the tree was a sapling did it ever dream of ever becoming anything else besides a tree. Maybe it had always dreamed of becoming a raspberry bush that flirted with everything that ever passed by it or maybe when the tree was young it always dreamed of being a rain cloud so it could see the entire forest from on high. How old was the tree when it finally realized that it would always be stuck being a tree? How many years after that did the tree come to peace with the reality of "once a tree - always a tree?"

Did the tree feel like it was part of a community with the other trees? Did it talk to the other trees about the weather? Was it all a competition to see who could be the tallest tree? Did the tree feel any petty jealousy toward the other trees that towered over it? Or did this tree cheer the other trees on as they climbed higher and higher. I guess what I really wanted to know is if the tree had ever fallen in love. I know you'll say "no"

UNTIED

because we don't like to put emotions on non-humans.

A bartender once asked how I would like my whiskey and trying to be clever, I said "Angry." This response led to a very long one-sided conversation where I was told that liquids don't feel anything. Which, of course, makes sense until the bartender told me that he was pissed that he forgot to bring his charger because his "phone was about to die." *Oh, so I see how it is. You phone can feel the sting of death but my whiskey (served neat) can't have a moment to be angry. You just get to pick and choose who gets to feel things? Whatever. You just lost your 20 % tip.*

I sat alone by this fallen tree for another twenty minutes and eventually I started wondering if it saw a tunnel of bright light at the exact moment the life force in it drained away. Was it greeted by a bunch of other trees who had passed away before it did? If I had to guess I would suppose that there isn't an afterlife for trees. I wish there was.

If I could be God for an hour or two, I would make one. It would be like a never-ending Arbor Day where trees are treated to a constant soft rainstorm and a massage of moss and midnight breeze. If I could build a paradise for fallen trees it would be in a place where they could all sit together and recite some slam poetry and not feel like they had let their parents down. Wait...that's me. Sorry.

I observed an army of black and red ants crawl all over the poor dead tree like they owned it. They were so busy building a nest in the corpse of the tree so they could live out their little any lives.

I closed my eyes and imagined that I was one of the ants.

"This tree is the entire world. This tree is the entire world. This tree is the entire world," I would say over and over while I carried on with my super important ant business.

Little did I know that the tree was coming back from the dead to offer me one last piece of advice. It would be like the movie "Ghost" but without any of the sexy pottery scenes or overacting.

UNTIED

"Tiny ant," the tree would whisper to me.

"Tree?" I would ask. (in case you were wondering my any voice sounded like Antonio Banderas)

"Tiny ant, I have come back from the great nothingness that awaits all trees when they die to bring you back a message."

"Okay - make it quick though, I have to check in with the other ants soon or they will forget about me."

Then the tree would say something that would later drive me into utter madness.

"Tiny ant, quit building your world on dead things."

With that the tree died again and I was left shaken. It was a comment so sinister that I would leave the ant colony and crawl into the first spider web I could find.

It was then that I quit imaging like I was an ant - but the sick feeling in my stomach remained.

Where am I building my world? Am I nesting in a dead tree trunk? Am I hanging my hat in a graveyard? Am I searching for life among ancient ruins?

Suddenly I stopped asking so many questions about the tree that had fallen, and I started directing the focus of my inquiries on myself.

Alone in the forest I started to cry.

Once a John Roedel - always a John Roedel.

Nobody heard me fall in the woods.

I guess that answers that question

My wife returned and took me by the hand to lead me out of the woods. We drove home that afternoon.

UNTIED

Temporary Us

give me the courage to

remember that I'm a tourist

in this world and when I

must board the train

to remember that

nothing comes with me

when I leave

customs gets it all

I don't get to take any souvenirs with me

everything must go into the bins

this is one of those resorts that doesn't

let me take anything with me

when it's time for me to go

no postcards of all the little villages I stayed while I was here

no magnets with pithy little wisdoms about hope or cats

no gold coins with ghostly presidents on their faces

no books that I pretended I was reading when you walked by

no maps that never kept me from getting lost in the woods

no grudges that I've kept fresh in my hotel ice bucket

no regrets that I watch in the movie theatre every night

no commemorative t-shirts about the time I won a twitter fight

I will leave it all behind

nothing that I'm clinging to in my hands

gets to come with me because

UNTIED

the place where I come from

has no need for such things

when the train whistle blows

and my vacation comes to an end

I will drop everything and leave everything behind

everything

except for my

thoughts of you

they are coming with me

I'll smuggle my memories of you

in the back pockets of my soul

and only let them out once I cross

the border that exists between

dust and spirit

I'll hold the last kiss you will give me

under my tongue until the coast is

clear and I can open my mouth

to let it out so it can turn into a

bright blue butterfly

the closer I get to the end of

my vacation

the less I want to take back home

with me

except my thoughts of you

they get to come

and when your vacation

comes to an end

and you must

UNTIED

follow the great whistle

and you must
unclench your hands
and let everything go

and you have to board
the train to the next place

don't fret
I'll meet you when you
walk off the train

look past the rolling steam
or the ribbons of glowing
stardust and you'll see me
standing right on the platform

JOHN ROEDEL

I'll be the one covered in

bright blue butterflies

and holding up a sign that reads:

"I never forgot you."

Therapy Taps

Tap. Tap. Tap. Tap. Tap. Tap.

Taptaptaptaptap. Tap. Tap.

It only took five minutes into our first session for my new therapist to become bored with me. I was just another meatball spinning my yarn of midlife clichés and cautionary tales. She had heard my sappy lyrics sung by better singers a hundred times before.

Tap. Tap. Tap. Taptaptaptap. Tap.

She kept tapping her pen on the notebook that she was using to pretend like she was taking detailed notes on about whatever it was that I was saying to her. I couldn't blame her. I had even stopped listening to myself.

Or perhaps the tapping of the pen was some sort of secret hypnosis that she was using on me to entrance me into sharing more than I had planned on. Maybe the pen was being used like a stopwatch. I became concerned that eventually she would get me to believe I was a penguin with mommy issues. I wondered if I would come to twenty minutes later standing naked on her desk holding her stapler between my legs like it was my little penguin egg I was protecting.

Then I decided that she was probably just using the tapping of her pen as a way of staying awake while I droned on about whatever weird stuff I say whenever I know that I'm being analyzed. I am terrible at small talk. I'm even worse at therapy talk.

As a performer there is no worse feeling than when you think that you have lost your audience.

"Uh huh," she said.

UNTIED

Tap. Tap. Tap.

"And how does that make you feel?" she asked. *Tap. Tap. Taptaptaptaptaptaptap.*

"What do you wish you could have done differently?" *Tap. Tap. Tappity. Tap.*

At one point I told her that

Silence is one of my

favorite sounds

and that perhaps

the lesson that I'm

here on Earth to

learn is that there

is a beautiful

power in solitude.

That maybe I'm at

my most peaceful

when I am

sitting alone in an

empty bathtub

in an empty house.

Her pen stopped. She looked at me over the notebook as if for the first time. It was quiet. We both absorbed what I was saying. I was even taken aback by it. This wasn't anything I had ever uttered out loud before.

I had finally said something that she found interesting.

She broke the silence:

UNTIED

"John, aren't you afraid that someday you will become an island?"

I bit my thumbnail for a moment.

An island?

"I hope so," I replied.

"Why do you want to be an island?"

I took another chew on my thumb. How could I explain this to her in a language that she could understand! I needed to choose my words with care. I feel finally had a captive audience.

With as much conviction as I could find I *said:

I want to be an

island because

I've long suspected that

mercy is an ocean

and I want to be

surrounded by it

on every side.

(* I probably said something far less poetic.)

After I was done talking, we both sighed very loudly for two very different reasons.

She was bored again.

&

I was relieved.

"Go on..." she said

tap

Tap tap taptap tap tap

UNTIED

The Wizard Of The Line

waist deep in The Yampa

moving water

pulling on my

grade school legs

inviting me into

the current

for a quiet baptism

of silt and weed

I don't go

I'm too busy

watching my

father cast lines

and spells

with the worms

I helped him select and

dig out from the mud

twenty minutes earlier

holding my father's beer

while he performed

his magic trick of

pulling rainbow trout

out of his dark moving

hat that surrounded us

UNTIED

the worms died

so that my dad

and I could live

forever in this moment

he was a wizard of

turning water into cutthroats and

conjuring creatures from the deep

onto his hook

it was all choreographed

perfectly

the stoic father -

the wide-eyed son -

the flicking line -

the dancing bugs -

the freezing current -

the gasping minnows -

the eye of God watching from the mountains -

the whispering reeds -

the crying birds -

the painted pumpkin sky -

the hunt -

the prey -

the pull of the river -

the splash of time on my face

&

UNTIED

the taste of memory lingering on my tongue

Chase It

if you want to

honor creation

seek it

out /

just know

that

the universe

is still cooling

better hold it by

the edges /

gaze straight

into the spiral

and then fall

straight in /

become friends

with a faraway nebula

then write the topsoil

a love letter /

it's all the

UNTIED

same /

it's all pure

magic /

it's all

lyrics

to the same song

of creation /

Phantom

vacant storefront eyes

peering into a crystal ball

of tomorrow

that only you can see

half-parted lips

offering no passage

from the whip and toil

of your unrelenting past

the zero expression on

your face that reads like

a blank check for an

overdrawn account

UNTIED

the slouch in your shoulders

that carries the weight of a

natural disaster that

only affects you

"Earthquake, party of one?"

I know the look on your face you wear like

a thin-stringed mask that

cuts the skin behind your ears

just enough to turn saltwater

into a truth serum

it's the adorned expression

of hopelessness and surrender

it's the unspoken cry for help

that only somebody who has been

carved open like a spaghetti squash

can understand

I see you

even when

you can't see yourself

UNTIED

Mother of Exiles

nobody talks to the old lady anymore

not really

adults offer her a smile and a

wave as they shuffle on by

with their busy lives

children looking at her through

three-inch screens

everybody taking pictures

to prove that they once saw

the old lady the water

JOHN ROEDEL

the tour guide warned us that

if we stay too long, we might suffer to

hear the crazed ramblings she mutters

under her breath

on a constant loop

but none of it ever really makes any sense

something about the ancient lands

blah blah and storied pomp's

and a little bit about tired masses

yearning to breathe free blah blah

and if you linger a while you will hear the old lady bemoan

through pursed trembling lips

UNTIED

a rift or two on the

homeless or tempest-tost

or a soft cry about a

lifted lamp something or other

it's all a bit too nonsensical for those of us

passing by to make any sense of it

it's all a bit too much antiquated nonsense

it's all a bit of old-world foolishness coming from a stony ghost

it's all a bit or a riddle that is lost in time and relevance

every now and then a person will

kneel beside her sketch

her with charcoal hoping to someday

JOHN ROEDEL

be famous

after all she was once the headliner

for the big show

a lifetime ago

she was the patron saint of

our great melting pot

experiment

she's the former matriarch of

a hopeful welcoming

she used to be

The First Lady of

UNTIED

needful people

that was a different age

that was before we

made a god out of

division

now she is considered

just another

old lady asking

about the whereabouts

of her lost children

"do you know where my kids are?"

JOHN ROEDEL

"I can't leave....my children will be visiting me at any moment."

"Have you seen my babies?"

nobody has the heart to tell her

that her children are gone

and they aren't coming back

so, we just smile and lie:

"you'll see them soon."

knowing that we won't actually

let them come

because her children scare us

UNTIED

"Okay," she replies softly

"I'll just wait here a little longer.

I can't wait to see my little ones again."

the consensus is that the old lady

is suffering from dementia

that she

has no idea

what she is talking about

that she is lost in time

I happen to think something

rather different

JOHN ROEDEL

that this NEW COLOSSUS

still has her wits about her

that this MOTHER OF EXILES

has a few tricks still up her repainted sleeves

I believe that

the old lady in the water

is just holding her breath

waiting for a time when

until fear is no longer the

currency of the age

until the dog whistle of "Protecting our culture"

UNTIED

has lost its melodic pitch

and on that day

her beacon hand will glow anew

and her mild eyes will become

a lighthouse once again

and this mighty woman

will rise from her

slumber and guide het lost

children back to our

sea-washed sunset gates

once again

and she will

JOHN ROEDEL

hold them

against her

thundering heart

until every chained fence

becomes a rose-woven arch

and on that day

we won't be able

to slide on past her

AND ON THAT DAY

she will

not be ignored

UNTIED

Spoons and Starlight

while

my spoon is

slowly stirring

a lobster bisque

in an overpriced

Restaurant

there is

a star is burning

into its own heart

and wrapping

time around itself

like a wool blanket

a hundred million

light years away

we are both

kissing cousins

of the same

symphony

of creation

whose time

has come

we are both collapsing

lights

UNTIED

a dying man

with paper skin

&

a dying body

of incandescent fire

dimming separately

yet together

twins

of the

same

groaning fate

we share different hospice nurses

yet the same universal bed

two fading souls

trying to find meaning

in their final act

trying to force

themselves to be

meaningful for

one last time

before it's too late

before we both go dark

before the great winter

UNTIED

stir

stir

burn

burn

can you hear my spoon, starlight?

we are brothers

of a shared

coming apocalypse

together we pray

for just one more

chance to burn

bright

JOHN ROEDEL

Every Empty Space

the fan above me

is louder than

the silence that

surrounds me

the night sky

is seducing

the sun

with one purple

wink at a time

God waits behind

the curtain

UNTIED

I've drawn

to whisper a

secret to me

that everybody else

already knows

"Every empty space

is a vessel for

an amazing grace."

the floorboards are

now in shadow

and begin to creak

footsteps

JOHN ROEDEL

all around

the angels dance

unseen

but their scent

lingers

part sage part cinnamon

part lilacs part honeycomb

the fan

labors on

above me

while I

disappear

into the mystic

underneath

UNTIED

Polaroid

hold me by the edges

until I develop

into something

that slightly resembles

how you would

like to remember me

The Tardiness of Signs

The predawn sky was silent and empty. It seemed like a perfect time for me to go outside and bother it again.

"Excuse me, I need a sign that things are going to work out." I requested up into the canvas of heaven that was mixing itself from grey to orange.

Nothing happened. I gave it a few more moments to give my words a chance to find their way to the proper divine authorities. Still nothing. Maybe the angels were sleeping in. Maybe they weren't taking me seriously. How lame of them.

I cleared my throat and tried again. This time with a deeper voice and with a little more force to it. I decided that I needed to scrap the word "need" and replace it with "deserve" - that should get the job done.

"I deserve a sign that things are going to work out for me."

I liked the way I sounded. I sounded official. Like a plastic surgeon asking his teenage caddy for a three wood on the 13th hole.

I got no response. Zero. Nada. Zilch. Not even a squeak from a waking robin that I could act like was a message from the spirit world.

How rude.

It was time to get serious. I took off my shoes and walked out further out into my backyard. The grass was wet with cold dew between my toes. The last time I remember being barefoot in the grass was as the cemetery last spring when I decided to have a Jimmy John's picnic with my headstone family. There is something very strange about the way cemetery grass rests under my feet. It felt sacred. Like I was being planted in time. Like there were roots wrapping around me. Like my hobbit-like feet were being washed by the ghosts of those I always came to seek forgiveness from. Like I was being transported from the physical to the ethereal.

The grass in my lawn didn't feel that way. It just felt like regular grass. It didn't help that right next to my feet was a recent fecal offering my dog had left overnight. That didn't add to the mystical ambiance I was hoping for.

The sun was starting to color the sky with a deeper blue, so I knew that I needed to get on with this whole episode before my family would wake up and see me standing in the backyard talking to nobody in particular - like a person who was starting to lose their mind. Which would be a totally fair assumption on their part.

UNTIED

I had recently begun to consider that it was becoming a very real possibility that I was, in fact, starting to have a very loose grip on my sanity. Everything I thought I knew about life was starting to come into doubt.

I had always thought of myself as a tightly wound ball of knots. But now...now I was unraveling into a spool on the ground.

I was becoming untethered to the person that I thought I was. It wasn't as if I was falling apart like a puzzle that could be reassembled. It was like I was shedding parts of me that I knew would never quite fit back in where they fell from. It was more than a maniac breakdown. It was a collapse in slow motion. It was like being in a car wreck that took a decade to complete. The car just kept flipping and flipping and flipping and flipping...and flipping.

It was a shitty way to live.

Now there I was standing with my arms outstretched in my backyard talking to the sky like he was a loan officer. Asking for a payday advance of mercy. Asking for just a taste of clemency. Asking for just a sliver of hope that I could fashion into a stick sword that I could try and scare my despair away with.

Where was God? Where were the intervening saints and angels that I was promised by my Catholic School teachers? Where were the olive branch chomping doves at the end of the flood? Where were the signs from heaven that I could swaddle myself up in like a blanket?

The signs weren't anywhere to be seen. Just like yesterday and the day before and the day before that. I had been getting up before daybreak for a couple weeks in hopes that I could catch God on the way to work to offer my lamentations. It was almost like God was taking a different route in order to avoid bumping into me.

After about ten minutes of listening and waiting for a callback from the divine I began to shake. I was getting cold. Not just in my feet or in my knees - but in my soul. It was starting to come to me in waves that perhaps God would never answer me.

Shake.

Shake.

Shake.

It was time to give up on this. It was time to quit asking the empty sky for help. It was time for me to grow up. I stretched out my arms one last time like a shorter and fatter version of Moses and cried out.

"I need a miracle!"

I didn't sound like myself. The tone of my voice sounded like a guttural yelp of a man who was feeling the unpleasant sensation of unraveling into a pile of string.

I took a deep breath and began to cry.

From just beyond the atmosphere above I heard the softest of voices respond.

"Miracle granted."

I could barely hear it. It was like a phone call with terrible reception from a friend who was on a work trip on Pluto. It was the faintest of whispers. It was the gentlest of statements. It was part of a song and part velvet.

UNTIED

I stopped unraveling for a moment in order to ask:

"What miracle? Where is it?"

No response. I wouldn't get another one.

I breathed in deeply again and felt the warm sting of my tears on my cold face.

There it was.

The answer I was looking for.

The signs

The miracles

The messages

everything I was waiting for

existed in my breathing

JOHN ROEDEL

lived in my tears

I was reminded that

every breath I take is a miracle

every breath I take is a sign

every breath I take is the message

that my life isn't over yet

that there is still an adventure to be lived

every tear on my face

every scar on my heart

every crack on my heart

are the proof that I haven't given up

UNTIED

And that I am stronger than I think I am

The sky was now royal blue. The sky was now teeming with birds. The trees begin to dance with the rising breeze. The silence was gone.

sunlight started peeking

in between the gaps

sunlight started reminding

that I still had some time

left

sunlight started to hold

me like a newborn

JOHN ROEDEL

shake

shake

shake

My heart was racing

My tears were racing

My breath was racing

I was racing

It was all a miracle

it was all a sign

that I still had some life left in me

I went back inside and slept. My wife later asked how our bed became filled with wet grass. I told her it was a sign that we were going to be okay. She looked at me funny.

UNTIED

I didn't blame her.

Her Rainbow

you are my favorite

color

and you change hues

every day

sometimes you are my

blue ocean inviting me

to an adventure that

exists just beyond

the reef I built last year

sometimes you are my

JOHN ROEDEL

orange sunset calling me

back home before the wolves

come out to feed

sometimes you are my

black midnight wrapping

me up tight in your bedsheets

to keep my scars

from leaking all over the floorboards

sometimes you are my

red sparrow serenading me

with an ancient song that

the angels taught you

when you slept under

UNTIED

the trees

sometimes you are my

purple Lent teaching me

that I am at my strongest

during my most shadow-clad

weakest hour

sometimes you are my

yellow sunflower jetting

up out of the weeds to offer

me a passing vision of mercy

and a delicate fragrance of hope

sometimes you are my

pink frosting that lingers

on the corner of my lips

long after you kiss me goodnight

sometimes you are my

watermelon comet that arrives

in the darkness of my closed eyes

like a mystery I'm desperate to solve

sometimes you are my

grey concrete casting all

of my memories in my mind

like handprints in the driveway

sometimes you are my

UNTIED

amber covering me in

your unbreakable strength

and your delicate beauty

sometimes you are my

white translucent telescope

asking me to keep searching

for a God who sometimes gets

hidden behind a nebula

it's all a bit of a cliché

but you are my

box of colored

pencils

JOHN ROEDEL

filling in the gaps

in my heart with

your brilliant tones

shading my untouched

areas of my life with

your saturated paints

you are the

chromatic

artist of my

world

coloring every inch

of my horizon with

your loveliness

UNTIED

The Hole in Me

I was born with

a hole

in

the upper

chamber

of my

heart

they call

it a murmur

I call it foreshadowing

Days Of

these are the days for

short speeches and

long instrumentals

these are the days for

frozen mouths and

dancing fingers on catgut

these are the days for

turning all the marks

we have dug into our

arms into violin strings

these are the days for

listening to the soft song

UNTIED

being sung to us by

the lights in our veins

these are the days for

believing in music

more than in humankind

these are the days for

falling in love under a

blanket of warm octaves

and tangled feet

these are the days for

forgetting the lyrics

we were taught by

people who were

afraid that we might

JOHN ROEDEL

write out our own

these are the days for

deciding what kind

of instrument we

want to be for the world

these are the days for

letting a piece of

sheet music be the

only map we need

to make it back home

to each other

these are the days for

holding bows instead

of grudges

UNTIED

these are the days for

falling in love all over

again with the harmony

of the breeze in the

old pines

these are the days for

being taken in by the

invisible conductor

inviting us into to

be a part of the symphony

these are days for

rhyme and rhythm

and sonatas and strings

JOHN ROEDEL

these are the days

for miracles and melodies

not speeches

UNTIED

MORE THAN BREATHING

You asked me yesterday how I have survived my mental illness for as long as I have. I didn't know how to answer you without looking like a sock sniffing creeper - but I've since decided that this information may very well save your life someday.

Here is how I survive:

I never told you this before but a few years ago I learned how to breathe through the crown of my head whenever I'm in the middle of one of those classic midnight panic attacks. I have found that my lungs aren't as reliable as the invisible hole in my cranium when it comes to supplying my body with oxygen.

This all sounds mad - I know. I know. I know.

When the darkness comes for me and I can't catch my air I have learned how to breathe in light. The science of how I do this is a bit suspect, though without discovering it, I would have been featured in a paid obituary long ago.

Here is what you do when Despair Cobra slithers up into bed with you and coils itself around your throat.

Lay back on your pillow. Close your eyes. Tight as you can. Seriously. Pinch the tears out the corners until they race back behind your head. It's like making warm lemonade - but it's a little more bittersweet.

Then you must fold your hands across your heart. I know it feels like a dozen wild horses are charging under your ribs. Don't worry, I feel that way too all the time.

Once your hands are resting on the rave of your heart, I want you to imagine that you are the last living

UNTIED

being left alive on Earth. Everything else is gone. Yes, even the cockroaches. It's just you and the deep ache of abject solitude.

Then I want you to think about what the edge of the universe looks like. Picture it however you want. For me it looks like a big blue wave that stretches in every direction that is still expanding out. Like a fat ripple in a still lake that paints a hundred million-star fields in its wake.

How does your universe edge look like? I hope it's beautiful. If it isn't - go ahead and redecorate it so it honors what the womb of new life looks like.

It's a mess.

It's chaotic.

It's churning energy.

It's all divine.

Go visit the edge of your universe. Don't worry about how you got there. Sometimes a journey can happen to us without our consent. It happens. I once found myself in Santé Fe before I knew I had ever gotten in a car. I'm pretty sure it was because of all The Sudafed I had been taking.

Anyway.

Whenever I visit the lip of the universe, I can hear the groans of creation still at work. Do you?

Sometimes I can smell the untouched grass of a slew of new baby Edens. It is like being in a hushed and endless maternity ward of newborn terraforming planets.

UNTIED

Welcome to the cradle of everlasting. Isn't it wonderful?

Then I want you to imagine that right there on the edge of infinity there is the smallest star anybody has ever seen. In fact, you could hold it in your hand if you wanted to. The star is part swimming goldfish and equal measure Fourth-of-July sprinkler.

The tiny star loves humming. Stay with me here. I know that it all sounds bonkers. The star is humming a song that you haven't heard since before you were born. I can never quite remember the lyrics to my song, but I always remember that some of it is about how pure nothing can become something and how darkness can become a bonfire with a snap of a finger or a wink from a bunny rabbit. It's a song about how fear can become love and division can transform into community in a single moment of laced fingers.

"What are you doing so far from home?" the star will ask you.

You say, "Because I can't breathe when I'm at home."

"Oh, well, that's because you are using your mouth."

Before you can respond the star will become a single ray of brilliant light. It will grab you by the hand and race you back through the universe. Past the burbling black holes. Past the swirling nebulas. Past the colliding galaxies. Past the crimson lizard king on Europa. Past the long-abandoned satellites being pulled into the deep. Past the coal scented atmosphere.

Right back through the roof of your house and straight into the invisible hole in your head.

UNTIED

You might hear a sound that sounds just like somebody snapping right next to your ears. That is simply the noise that your soul makes when it finally wakes up. Once I heard a plate breaking. That was just my ego being obliterated.

Don't fret - it's all normal.

Well, it's as normal as any of this can be.

It is sort of impossible to explain how you will feel when you come back home from the fringe of creation through the top of your skull. It's more than relief. It's more than feeling at peace. It's more than being hopeful. It's more than anything you have ever felt before.

Likely you'll notice your heart slowing down. You will feel the tears dry. You will feel like you are doing more than just surviving. You will feel like you are finally connected to who you have always meant to be.

You will feel the hand of God on your back.

It's like breathing

but it's more than

breathing.

It's living.

And sometimes if you're lucky…

you will discover the remnants of a little star on the palm of your hand - a thin coat of stardust

Soon after that you will feel your lungs push up and down. The world will come back to you. You aren't alone anymore.

UNTIED

This is how you survive.

Y & U

I want to start unfolding

and then unfold some more

and then to never stop unfolding

I want my

days to be

like an ancient

map that gives

me directions to

a buried

box of forgotten

gold coins

every day I want

to be unfurled only

JOHN ROEDEL

a little bit more to give

me just enough clues

on how to make it to

the next waypoint

I don't want to

ever reach

the part on the map

where X marks

the spot

I find the letter X relentlessly boring

the answers are

never as fun

as the questions

UNTIED

I am seduced by Y

Y am I still here?

Y is my heart so full?

Y is this monster under my bed?

Y is God hard to find?

Y is the Universe singing to me?

Y have we become entangled together?

I want to live

In the adventure

of the present

moment

I want my life to

unfold a little today

and a little more tomorrow

and a little more every

day that follows

I don't want to win the lottery

I want to live

like a river

whose bends

are even

a mystery

to the water

that flows in it

I want to follow the Y

without concern of the X

God,

keep unfolding me

until I am a checkered

UNTIED

thin picnic blanket

that covers the hill

of my last supper

God,

let me be

more about

the question

than I am the

solution

unfold me

unfold me

unfold me

but if You don't mind

just

a little bit at a time

JOHN ROEDEL

Blossoms of Absence

grief made me a garden

and allowed the dandelions

to wildly grow

grief laid me in weeds and

kindly told me to wait for

the wind to blow

with every new gale

came a parade of

fresh blowing seeds

with every autumn gust

UNTIED

I could feel a little

bit of my hurt leave

out in the air

went the pieces

of my poor heart

out in the sky

I watched my pain

turn into untethered art

grief isn't meant

for us to clutch up

or to tightly hold

JOHN ROEDEL

grief is the way that

our lost loved ones

story can be told

to share their path

and their spirit

and their lives

is exactly how

grief allows their

memory to survive

grief is a garden

full of things

that we thought were dead

UNTIED

but death isn't

final because it's

only our skin that we shed

so, lay me down softly

in a thousand yellow dandelions

and all around me they will grow

until the forever wind comes

to tell the story of my life

when it's finally my time to go

JOHN ROEDEL

The Importance of Not Winning

I think I lost

you the moment

that you started

to fall in love

winning

can I tell you something?

there is no winning

because there has

never been anything

to win

UNTIED

there are no medal ceremonies

there are no jackpots

there is no Boardwalks with a hotel

there is no bullseye

relax,

there isn't a game

that you need to win

there is only us

and the holy delicate

strings that

we tie between each

other to keep us

floating up into oblivion

JOHN ROEDEL

I'll say it again

we are tied to each other

we are laced up

together by

common strings

how can you win that sort of game?

there is only

us and the way

we help each other

survive between sunsets

UNTIED

it's not a race

it never was

we are all tortoises

ambling down

the same track

together toward

the same

finish line

of eternity

there is nothing to win

but if you aren't careful

there is everything to lose

don't ignore the itch under

your skin telling you there

is more to this organic ride

than just winning

there is community

there is healing

there is us

there are the strings

that tie us to one another

winning won't

welcome you

UNTIED

on your first day

in the great beyond

but, I will

please pay attention to this next part,

it's time to start listening

to your heart again

it's not too late

I swear

I'm tugging at our common strings

Can't you feel it?

JOHN ROEDEL

The Way of Kindness

If I become

a book in

my next life

let my story

be called

"*The Way of Kindness*"

It will be 65000 pages

of the same sentence

over and over

"Don't spend your days sharpening your life into

a spear because ALL wars EVENTUALLY come to an end."

That is only the story

UNTIED

I want to tell in all

my different lifetimes

Regardless of form

let me tell my story another

hundred thousand times

in whatever skin I am laid

down in

Let me be a book held by children

Let me be a softly played piano

Let me be a graffiti wall in Boston

Let me be a dove over the ocean water

Let me be a lantern in the darkest midnight

Let me a child holding a rose up to a gun

Let me be a rainbow after the storm

Let me be a single burst of sun on hard ice

JOHN ROEDEL

Regardless of how I incarnate

Let me tell the only story

I was born again and again to tell

UNTIED

The Way of Kindness

"Don't spend your days sharpening your life into a spear because ALL wars EVENTUALLY come to an end. Don't spend your days sharpening your life into a spear Because ALL wars EVENTUALLY come to an end. Don't spend

your days sharpening your life into a spear because ALL wars EVENTUALLY come to an end. Don't spend your days sharpening your life into a spear....."

UNTIED

Teenage Therapy Club

I was 16 years old

and it was my turn

to share with the

circle of fellow

misfits

I had been invited

to take part in an

after school program

that I was told was

for "creative" kids

JOHN ROEDEL

it was explained

to me by my parents

that this program

would be a fantastic experience

to help me explore

and develop my "imagination"

at that point in my life

my imagination

was my best friend

I was born

into a family

of scientists

and deep thinkers

UNTIED

I wasn't one of them

I was the intellectual

fifth wheel in a family

of four

instead of doing my algebra

I scribbled short stories about

coma patients and talking statues

on the back of my homework sheets

instead of memorizing historical facts

I practiced my standup comedy

in the mirror that I would use the next

day at the high school lunch table

I wrote poetry when

I should have been

writing college essays

the older I was getting

the less I was relying on

what I thought

I was all about how I felt

when it became clear

to me that I just didn't

care about maintaining

UNTIED

the whole love triangle between

myself, my heart and my brain

I let my brain file for emancipation

it left without fanfare

and packed

up my academic career

with it

which understandably

bothered my parents

who valued the educational system

the way a farmer values rain

JOHN ROEDEL

my parents wanted

me to have a plan for my life

and I wanted life to be a constant

surprise party

why worry about four years from now

when I had a sandwich in my hand?

who cares about the job market in a decade

when I could lay naked in the bathtub and listen

to Michael Stipe sing about gardening at night?

my parents believed in concrete

UNTIED

and I believed in sand

we were at an impasse

that is why they

"encouraged" me

to attend the after school

program for "creative" kids

I became suspicious

when I walked into

the first meeting

and discovered

that there were no

items that a "creative"

kid might use

there were no pencils

or paper

or paint brushes

or instruments

or glue

there were just chairs

arranged in a circle

the other kids

who were at the

meeting had the same

look in their eyes

UNTIED

as I did

the look

of a person

who had

surrendered to

their heart

and the expense of

their brain

we were a collection

of kids who were bookended

with quotation marks

like they were our diagnoses

JOHN ROEDEL

"emo"

"different"

"quiet"

"funny"

"weird"

"outsider"

"creative"

it was all code

for being kids who

were considered at risk

my allegiance to my

heart had become a liability

UNTIED

to me in the eyes of the adults

the meeting opened

with a song by Cyndi Lauper

"I can see your true colors..."

they almost saw my vomit

within a few moments

it became clear to me

that we weren't there to

explore our creativity

we were there to be

evaluated to make

sure, we weren't

on the highway to

self-harm

it was evident that

we were considered

kids who needed fixing

we were the boxes

of crumpled cereal

that gets shoved to

the back of a grocery shelf

the theme of the meeting

UNTIED

weren't as much about creativity

as it was more about

explaining how we thought

that we had gotten broken

but I didn't feel broken

I just felt miscast

for the role I had been given to play

I viewed my life as an unfolding

river

where behind every bend

there was another unexpected

valley to explore

how in the hell

was I going to

explain that?

29 years later

I still can't

we all sat in a circle

with our heads bowed

down waiting for our

turn to explain

our perceived brokenness

UNTIED

it was my turn

and I prayed for

an earthquake to swallow

the whole room up in one

gulp

"Why do you think you are struggling in so much in school," my guidance counselor asked.

she wanted to see my true colors

I squirmed in my seat

and stared over her head

at the bright red exit sign

behind her

JOHN ROEDEL

I said something like profound like

"I dunno"

and tried to hide within myself

"Think about it," she pressed

I couldn't think about it

as I had let my brain

float out of my skull

years ago like a bright

pink birthday balloon

I stared back at her

UNTIED

and simply said

"Because school sucks. Can I go now?"

In that answer I became

a teenage cliché

of disconnected surliness

I wish I had said something else

since it was the answer that she was trained to respond to

I fell right into the trap of her well-intended script

she then lectured me on the importance of my education

and how I needed to take advantage of all the

opportunities in my life that I was blessed to have

and how I was letting down my parents

and what kind of job would I be able to get with that kind of attitude

and..and...and...and...

I nodded along

because she was singing a song

that I had heard all my life

it was a song called

"get your head out of the clouds"

the thing is I have always loved clouds

clouds are where the angels are

and possible UFO's

UNTIED

and the secrets of heaven

clouds are billowing and mysterious

and without form

which was exactly how I wanted to live my life

I wasn't interested in the answers of life

I was interested in the questions that had no answers

at the end of the meeting of "creative" kids

that I ever attended

I was given a piece of paper

that had a simple question on it

"Who do you want to be?"

JOHN ROEDEL

I never filled out the paper

because I didn't know

what I wanted to be

I still don't

not really

if anything,

I want to have a

heart made of cotton candy

that's it

I want a heart

that's

UNTIED

easy to pull apart

and to dissolve

away under the

the hot breath of

the present moment

I want to remove pieces of my confectionary

heart every day and place

it in your hands

and wait for you to consume it

and wait for you to understand me

Who do I want to be?

Understood

I guess that's it.

JOHN ROEDEL

Can I go now?

Beyond the Sprawl

maybe fences

don't ever keep

us from really getting

hurt

maybe borders

are just make believe

lines that we draw in the

dirt

maybe the barbed wire

we put up can cut us

UNTIED

whether we touch it or

not

maybe all this dividing

us into kingdoms is

what caused the land to

rot

maybe a gated community

is more of a prison than

it ever was really a

church

maybe the way forward

is to leave our tidy acres

and go on a lifelong

search

maybe God exists

outside of where we

built our tranquil little

dome

maybe a house built with

tinted windows and thick bricks

will never feel like a real

home

maybe just maybe

life is waiting for us

UNTIED

just beyond our safe

wall

maybe just maybe

mercy is waiting for us

in the wild of the glorious

sprawl?

The Point of Knots

I spent four days

trying to write

a poem about

knots

Nothing worked

It all felt cliché and over complicated

I wrote for hours

I filled up a half a notebook looking for twenty good words

UNTIED

I was stuck

Then it dawned on me

That's the whole point of knots

to keep everything together

and in their place

to keep us stuck

to keep us moored to the dock

to keep us in our dress shoes

to keep us tied to the fence

to keep us bound to the past

to keep us to keep us to keep us

I'm still stuck trying to untie my knotted tongue so I can explain all of this to you

I'm doing my best to write a poem about how I feel a knot in my stomach every time my phone rings

I'm doing my best to explain that I might need some help unknotting this coil of rope around my neck

I'm doing my best to explain to you that I'm trying to untie more knots in people than I give them

I'm doing my best to explain how I accidentally cast so many of my knots I put between us I in concrete

UNTIED

I'm doing my best to explain how I am trying to live a life that is knot free

I'm doing my best to explain the reason why I haven't worn shoes with laces in them for 30 years

I'm afraid of knots

There I said it

Thank God.

That's the poem in four words:

I'm afraid of knots

JOHN ROEDEL

That's what I've been

trying to say for days

That's what I've been

trying to say for pages

That's what I've been

trying to say for my

whole fucking life

UNTIED

Out of The Woods

come out of the woods

all the

people who love

you are still

waiting for you

at the last place

you were ever seen

you remember

where that is, right?

it's the clearing

where you ran into

the Forest those

JOHN ROEDEL

many years ago

they haven't moved

they are waiting

in the place

where the

trees kiss the

beginning

of the valley

they are waiting

to remind you

who you are

they are waiting

to cover your

scars in blessed oils

UNTIED

they are waiting

to teach you

all the lyrics

of your song

they are ready

to wash you

in a light that

you have never

felt before

come out of the woods

they have already

forgiven you

come out of the woods

The Logic of Trees

I hate arguing with trees.

"Did you know

that the light can make fingers

out of the shadows?" a grove of Aspens asked me as I walked by them.

I shook my head.

How stupid.

How ludicrous.

"Why would it do that?" I asked incredulously.

"So, it can to pick you up

when you're

on the ground," they replied.

Damn.

I hate arguing with trees.

UNTIED

Oh, My

On the mornings

when I'm afraid to

wake up

In my darkest hour I feel

you clutch my disquieted

hands while laying your

dandelion head on my spitfire heart

If you'd be so kind

can you try to feel all the words

that I cannot say to you

as I softly break apart

JOHN ROEDEL

I know it's hard to watch

but my trembling form is

a coded message

I need you to understand

Can't you recognize

this slow-motion

sadness of mine

was nothing that I had planned?

When we first met

I didn't know that my

stomach would become

a swarm of raging bees

UNTIED

nor did I ever predict

that my natural posture

would become me

crying on my knees

but the warmth

of your skin keeps

me from turning into

an abandoned ghost town

the gentleness of

your calming rainwater

keeps me from

burning this whole world down

JOHN ROEDEL

I am not my sadness

nor am I my melancholy,

or my anger, or my fears

I am not my inward shame

because you have kissed

me with kind lips,

lavished me with blessings

while reminding me of my own name

I will never be claimed

by depression because

I will belong to you,

my angel in blue jeans

UNTIED

you turned your life

into my lighthouse

and you silenced

all my midnight screams

so, as I slowly drift between

the bookends of surrendering to

my hungry madness

and my need to fight fight fight

just know that through my war

I can feel your hand laced in mine,

your tears falling;

and that you are bathing me in light

JOHN ROEDEL

oh, my shelter in the tempest

oh, my dove among crows

oh, my dawn despite midnights

you are my refreshing remedy

oh, my constant among uncertainty

oh, my patient burning north star

oh, my love song from heaven

you are my sweet melody

I am still here

on this spinning rock

because of

the celestial gift that is you

UNTIED

I am not

afraid of waking up

anymore because you are

the waiting morning dew

Luna, Please Don't Go

Before you fall asleep, I need to tell you something. A couple of weeks ago, do you remember when you asked me what it is like to write something that I know people probably won't ever read. I tried to answer but I could tell that you lost interest.

Hold my hand while I try again.

There is a tree in the park close to our home that I visit a couple times a week. We have an arrangement. We tell each other our most delicate secrets without judgement. A while ago the tree told me something that I think will explain my writing process to you. Please stay awake while I explain.

The tree told me that has been madly in love with the moon for as long as it can remember. Even if the moon is invisible the tree can still feel it.

Every night as the moon passed overhead the tree would recite the same poem up to it.

Luna

Luna

UNTIED

please don't go

Luna

Luna

I love you so

Luna

Luna

I need to be saved

Luna

Luna

By your light I crave

Every night the moon

speeds on by

without saying a

single thing in response

Every night the tree

feels shattered

and falls asleep under

the contrails of the

passing moon glow

Every night the tree

says under his

acorn breath

"Never again."

The tree always means

no more moon gazing

no more poetry

UNTIED

no more being vulnerable

no more

Then the dawn

comes and the tree

starts to feel differently

and then the day

comes and the tree

forgives the moon

and then the night

comes and the tree

offers a soft psalm

"One more try..."

and the tree waits

for the darkened horizon

to light up again

for his love to return

and to pass over him

Luna

Luna

I love you so

Luna

Luna

Please don't go

Luna

Luna

UNTIED

I need to be saved

Luna

Luna

By your light that I crave

the tree calls out

to the moon

every night

and every night

the moon

passes

silently by

and every night

the tree

JOHN ROEDEL

gets hurt

and every next

day the tree

tries again

this is exactly what

writing feels like

it's the call

and the silence

it's the poetry

and the loneliness

it's the falling in love

and the falling to pieces

it's the heartbreak

UNTIED

and the forgiveness

it's the glimpse of light I can't reach

and the inevitable shadow that follows

it's the "never again"

and the "one more try"

writing is the call to

light that often goes unhear

it's chasing of

illumination

it's the patient vigil

for just one response

do you understand now?

does that make sense?

are you still awake?

JOHN ROEDEL

my love?

Seeds

I can feel
the ground shake
where they
buried you

under my
feet

you are
stirring

you are
scratching

your way
back

my love,

they buried

UNTIED

you

but they
forgot

that you
were

the seed
to

the prettiest
marigold

this world
will

ever fucking
see

dig
scratch
claw
your way

JOHN ROEDEL

back up to us

the fight
will worth
the bloom

someday
you will
cover this
town in the
color of your
courage

burst open
burst open
burst open

I can feel
the ground
shaking where
they buried you.

burst open
burst open

UNTIED

burst open

my lovely
marigold

burst open

right under me,

burst open

JOHN ROEDEL

I Understand

Whenever you
begin to cry

I stop talking
because I remember

that your tears don't
any have ears

When you cry

I close my mouth
like a basilica door
that is sealed the
moment that
the jubilee ends.

UNTIED

When you cry

I open my heart
so you can let go
of the trapeze
you are clinging to and
fall right down into
a gentle silence
of hushed compassion.

Let me catch you
with the net of
my eyes and the
softness of my hands.

Your sorrow is
not my open mic
night.

Your sorrow is
the call to

JOHN ROEDEL

hold you in the
quiet of sobs
your breaking heart.

Grief sometimes comes
as a spider crawling under
the door and sometimes
it comes as a bear rumbling
through the wall.

Let me hold your spiders
until they cover my fingers
in webs

Let me calm your bear
with my trembling arms
until it bows its head and
falls asleep in my lap.

The right words that
I need to say to you
are often inaudible.

God, if I must say

UNTIED

something to you
when you are fracturing
let it just be

"I understand"
over and over.

I understand
I understand
I understand
I understand
I understa-

JOHN ROEDEL

Say It

when you have

a heart so heavy

that you can't help

but sink into

your terrible sadness

there is only

one way out

just say the word

you know which

one I'm talking about

before you drown

UNTIED

in your melancholy
open your mouth
and scream the
most difficult word
that has ever existed

it's the one
word that will
invoke an army
of open-handed angels
to pull you from the
bottom of the lake

it's the one word
that will frighten
the cold voice in
your mind into
silence

it's the one word
that will require every
ounce of courage that
you have in order
to form it on your

JOHN ROEDEL

blue lips

it's the only word
that will save your
life

it's the most important
word you will ever know

please say it
please sing it
please scream it

scratch it into

my back if

you have to

before it's too late

just say it

UNTIED

the word is full of magic

just say it

we are all waiting
to swoop in

say it
say it
say it

just say HELP

please
please
please say it

JOHN ROEDEL

Lighthouses

Dear you,

A long time ago you asked me to tell you what unconditional love looks like. I didn't have an answer then.

I do now.

It was late in the day when my beloved raced against the sunset to come home to me. She breezed through the door and sat down next to me at our table that was covered in my damned notebooks that follow me wherever I go. She had come home to discover that both the house and I were half-lit and in complete disorder.

UNTIED

I was ashamed.

My beloved placed her hand on mine and asked me how I spent my day.

I was ashamed.

Softly I told her that the only thing I accomplished all day was writing another poem about an abandoned lighthouse that nobody will probably ever read.

Without hesitation she kissed my forehead and told me that she had never been prouder of me.

That is how I know what unconditional love is.

It comes without hesitation.
It comes with a kiss of peace.
It comes just before the sun sets.
It comes to help me get to the shore.
It comes with a light that cuts into the dark.

The thing is I can't quit writing about lighthouses but at least I know why that is now.

JOHN ROEDEL

I write about lighthouses because I live with one.

love, me

AWAY

I woke up this morning
to let you know I was
about to drift
up up up and away

not because I wanted to

the thing is,
I've been untethered
for so long

and I hate it
and I've fought it
and I'm scared of it

UNTIED

and I can't help it

and I'm
about to float

so very far

a
     w
          a
               y

but then you
rose from every
horizon to
remind me
that I'm not drifting
away

I never have been

I've been floating
straight
to

JOHN ROEDEL

you
this whole time

there is nowhere
for me to stray
that your light won't
find me

you are both
my departure
and my arrival

all passages
I float to
lead me right back
into the warmth
of your sol touch

what I never realized
until just now is that
you are just as untethered
as I am

we were born weightless

UNTIED

we were born to float

we were born as celestials

we were born to orbit each other

to dance
to float
to drift

anchored only to each other
with invisible strings

swaying together
exploring together
floating together

until forever
until forever
until forever

comes to make us
start all over again

ocarina

I was born with a hole in my heart
that kept my parents from having
a decent night of sleep for the
first year of my life

they would take turns
sitting next to my crib
every evening watching me
sleep to ensure that my
heart would remember
to keep beating

my dad would steady one
hand softly on my chest
and the other on one of his

UNTIED

cheap world war 2
spy novel he'd
likely be reading
and waiting for my mom to relieve
him for her shift at around 2 a.m.

every time I sneezed they thought
my heart would turn into dynamite

every time I
cried they waited for
death to slip in under the door to
collect their little boy

they were waiting for
the shoe other shoe
to drop

I was real-life
version of Russian roulette

it was only a matter
of time before the hole
in my heart would break

JOHN ROEDEL

theirs into pieces

my parents weren't
walking on eggshells

they were line dancing
on them

after I survived the first
year my parents started
to relax a bit around their
son with a holey heart

maybe he would make it
maybe he wasn't just a bomb of grief waiting to
detonate
maybe his story wouldn't just be all prologue
maybe his hole would be fine

still, my incomplete heart
was never far from their full attention

I remember on my
first day of elementary school

UNTIED

when my
mom showed up at lunch to
tell my teacher that I
had to sit on the bench
at recess because
you know...heart hole

so I sat
and watched everybody
chase each other

Stacy came over
to ask me to join
in the great
run with them

I can't remember her
last name
but I remember her long
jet black hair

"I can't," I said

"Why?" Stacey asked

JOHN ROEDEL

"I have a hole in my heart," I said

"Oh, sorry."

That was the response I usually
get whenever I tell people that
I'm unwell.

Oh, sorry.

What else is somebody
supposed to say
when I turn our small talk
into a confessional?

"Hello John."

"I'm broken."

"Oh, sorry."

The older I got, the less
my parents began to outwardly

UNTIED

fret about the gap in my ticker

they relaxed
but not really

they kept waiting
for the heartbreak to
show up

My heart with a hole in it
would only get brought
up when I let them down

which in hindsight was
a lot

it became a point of leverage for them

I was 22 when they
showed up at the door
of my college apartment

speaking in tandem

JOHN ROEDEL

"We saw your midterms."

"Uh huh."

"Why did you drop
out of that class?"

"Because it was stupid
and the professor didn't like
me and it was too hard and
I don't understand why I need
to take it and I just needed a
break from studying and
I will take it later and it's not
a big deal."

"You are failing
half of your classes."

"I like to look at it
like I'm passing half
of them."

"Don't be smart with us."

UNTIED

"Right."

"Are you going to
be able to graduate
from college this semester?

"Probably not."

"Do you know how
much we took care
of you when you
were a baby?"

"Yes, of course."

"Do you know
how many nights
we prayed for your
heart to not stop?"

"Yes, of course."

"Do you know how much stress you have caused us?"

JOHN ROEDEL

"Yes, of-"

"Do you know that
your brother is getting
his master's next week
and you can't even be bothered
to finish your undergraduate classes."

"I know..."

"You are really letting
us down. "

"I know - but -"

"Why are you doing this to us?"

"I think there is something
wrong with me. That's why."

long pause

"Oh, sorry."

UNTIED

then the three of us
said the worst thing
we could have
in that moment
in the doorway of my
college apartment:

nothing

we stood there is
silence

I had finally broken their
heart

their fretting and worrying
became fully realized

shoe met floor

what I couldn't explain to
them at the time was
that I had a second

JOHN ROEDEL

hole in me forming

that scared me a lot more

than my first one

this time the hole

was in my brain

the hole in my mind

was less of a murmur

and more like a monster

it was a hole

that wanted to

consume me whole

it was a hole

that had several

rows of crooked teeth

that left bite marks

on my stomach

whenever I tried to

get out of bed

I never told either of them

UNTIED

about it because they had
already worried their lives
away on me

I just closed the door and
they went back home and
I went back inside to
lay down in a dry
bathtub listening to
the holes in
my head and heart
write love letters
to each other

two years later
I was in Taizé, France
on a pilgrimage

I traveled there with
a church group
but in reality I was
there on my own

I had come around the

JOHN ROEDEL

world to talk to

God who had

apparently started

wearing camouflage

I had recently started

to experience a new

hole forming inside of me

this time it was in

an un-seeable place

inside of me

my soul

this hole hurt

the most

all the magic

and miracle

and joy of living

and faith

that I used to feel

were leaking out of me

UNTIED

and into the sky above

I had come around the
world to tell God to patch
me up

but I was met with the exact
same absence I had back
home

God never showed up
with a first aid kit

My dad had died
a month before

the experiences
I had surrounding
his death were still
laying heavy on me

I had so many
regrets that they
had to take turns

JOHN ROEDEL

tying themselves
to my back

so many unspoken words

which truth be told
was the genesis of
my trip to Taizé

I had come around the
world to tell God to tell
him I'm sorry I wasn't
a better son

but God wasn't accepting
my phone call

I could feel the hole
in my heart widening
and the one in my head
and the one in my soul
I was nothing but holes now

they would soon merge

UNTIED

and I would be gone

sitting there among
truly holy people
I was the holeyest of them all

there were people
from all walks of
life and faiths
sitting in the beautiful
candle lit temple

it looked the part
of where mystical
experiences take place
on a routine basis

during the day we
would labor around
the camp site

hundreds of us would be
cooking
cleaning rooms

JOHN ROEDEL

building structures

scrubbing bathrooms

and then four times a day

the bell would ring to call

is to temple where

we would sit there

long periods of either

silence or simple song

the songs were

usually just a line

or two of lyrics

that would be repeated

over and over

for 10-20 minutes

I sang the words

hoping I could

at the very least

brainwash myself

into believing things

would be okay

UNTIED

I didn't need God
to be real

I just needed to go
back believing that
God was real

I decided there was
a difference between
the two

I spent every session
for five days
singing for my life

hoping that the
words would make
a garden inside of me

but I had too
many holes for
rose bushes to
grow

JOHN ROEDEL

on my last night there
something happened

I remember the song
we were singing when
the old man next
grabbed my hand
and held it tightly in his

"Bless the Lord, my soul
And bless God's holy name
Bless the Lord, my soul
Who leads me into life"

He was crying;
actually sobbing is a better description
of what he was doing

it wasn't sorrowful weeping
he was crying with a wide smile
revealing his toothless mouth

I could feel the calluses
in his palm rub

UNTIED

against my smooth skin

I felt ashamed

the contrast between
the condition of our
hands felt like an indictment
of my life

it didn't seem to faze the old man
one bit as his hand kept squeezing mine
in rhythm to the song

"Bless the Lord (squeeze), my soul (squeeze)
And Bless God's (squeeze) holy name (squeeze)
Bless the Lord (squeeze), my soul (squeeze)
Who (squeeze) leads me (squeeze) me back into
(long squeeze) life.

The song went on for about ten minutes or so

I would like to say that I squeezed
his hand back
but I didn't

JOHN ROEDEL

I was uncomfortable
and distracted
his hands were very dirty
his robes were covered in mud
his body didn't smell very good
he appeared to be extremely poor

he kept crying
he kept squeezing
and I just wanted it to end

eventually it did

we all got up to leave
the old man was still holding my hand
and gave it one last super squeeze

I gave him the fakest smile I could produce
it was Oscar worthy
I then offered him a bow
like he was some sort of enlightened master

he shook his head

UNTIED

and poked me in the chest
hard

ow

and despite my
trying to back out
of it the man lurched
forward and hugged me

the only way to describe
the way this man held me
was to say it felt like I was
being swaddled by a hundred
million fireflies

there was an energy
in his unwashed arms

the base of my spine
was like a rocket that
wanted to take off

my skin tingled

JOHN ROEDEL

like every particle
inside of me was
getting a kiss from
heaven

I know that sounds
ridiculous

When we stopped
hugging I suddenly became
concerned that I was going to
pass out

I was going to be
one of those people
who hit the ground
after a faith healer
slaps them in a
white suit slaps them
upside the face with
some southern spirit

my body was shaking

UNTIED

the man poked my chest again
harder (ow) and said something to
me in a language I could not
understand

a lady about half his age
who had been sitting on the other
side of him the entire time
waved at me

she said in jumbled English
"Do you want to know
what he said?"

"Yes, of course."

"He said let all of the incomplete things is you and let them
become an instrument. Tie all your broken pieces
together and become a wind chime."

I smiled
this time it was real.

JOHN ROEDEL

With that the lady took the
old man by the hand and
they disappeared in the crowd.

My spine spoke up again:

Be an ocarina. An instrument whose many holes in
will turn the wind into music.

Be a wind chime. Bless the world with the gently
clanging sound of grace passing through you.

You are not a decoration. You are a wounded
apparatus of melody and song. Your gaps will hum
with spirit.

I was ready to levitate straight up through the roof of
the chapel. I was a kite begging to kiss a star field.

My spine went back to sleep - but the fire remained.

I asked the wind to turn the holes in me into music. I
begged grace to turn me into sound.

UNTIED

I sat back down to
sing on my own

and that's when the visions came

Bless the Lord (*I could see my parents sitting by my crib*)
my soul (*I could feel my dad's hand on my newborn chest*)
And Bless God's holy name (*I could rushing over to me whenever I cried*)
Bless the Lord (*I could see my mom wring her hands with worry on my first day of school*)
who leads us back to life (*I could see my parents wiping the tears from their face as I shut my college apartment door on them*)

Forgiveness washed over me

They loved me
They did their absolute best to protect me
They didn't know what to do with the holes forming in me
That's okay - because neither did I

JOHN ROEDEL

I was never a very good son to either of my parents

I asked God to tell my dad
that I was sorry
oh (so) sorry
oh (so) sorry
oh (so) sorry

I was assured that
my dad would get the message

It was in that moment
as I sat in a near empty
temple on the other side
of the world
that the gaping holes
in my heart
and my mind
and in my soul

all became an ocarina
and my wounds became wind chimes

and for one night I became the most beautiful song

UNTIED

that I've ever heard

and from that moment on, the conversation goes like this:

"Hello John."

"I'm broken."

"Oh, sorry."

"I'm not.

JOHN ROEDEL

Flowerpower

we put flowers on
mom's coffin
while I had one
pinned on my coat

we spent a summer placing
buttercups in the water just
to learn from them
how to effortlessly float

we give a bride a
bright bouquet
that she carries straight
down the long aisle

UNTIED

we give the suffering
an arrangement
to help them survive
their terrible trial

we are told to
smell the roses
and to look for
miracles every day

we are told that if
we plant a thousand
gardens than our world
won't feel as gray

I think most clouds
look like blossoms
that are ready to burst
with petals invisibly pink

I think I could write you a
a perfect love letter
if I could use warm nectar

JOHN ROEDEL

instead of cold ink

our world is covered
in topsoil made for lilacs
yet we spend all of
our time counting gold

I believe our world is a
humming sunflower microphone
waiting for your
life story to be bravely told

we give each
other a bundle of tulips
before the darkness
breaks us in two

we give each
other daisies
when it's time
to bid adieu

we shower our
bed in white orchids

UNTIED

when a lover
arrives in sweet lace

we make a blanket
out of wildflowers
as we lay in our
vulnerable embrace

in all of our years
and our days and
in every single one
of our sacred hours

we are just finding
reasons and excuses
to drown each other
in the most beautiful flowers

JOHN ROEDEL

The Shape of Love

don't you dare believe them

the shape of love
isn't a heart
with an arrow
running through it

that's a myth
that's a hallmark card
that's a shallow lake
that's a vein-less wrist
that's a crime scene

actually, my love,

UNTIED

the shape of love
is a wine glass
marked with your lipstick

the shape of love
is a billowing cloud
that lingers like ghost
over a lover's picnic

the shape of love
is the heaven—kissed hand of a newborn wrapped
around the finger
of her mom

the shape of love
is a warm bath
that has been made into
a makeshift chapel
adorned with candles
and floating rose petals

the shape of love
is a scarf
I found under the

couch that still

carries your scent

long after you

slipped away

the shape of love

is the teardrop

reclining on your fingertips

that you lifted off my

flushed cheeks

during one of my spells

the shape of love

is the formation

your mouth make when

you absolve me for

not recognizing the miracle

the shape of love

is the silhouette

of your body when

you walk in front of

the dripping moonlight

UNTIED

the shape of love
is a cold hand on a
fevered forehead

the shape of love
is a book of poetry
that vibrates whenever
we hold it to our chest

the shape of love
is the look on the
face of a child playing
in the snow for the
first time

the shape of love
is the foot prints
you left in the wet sand
after your kissed me
on my neck

the shape of love
is an old soul
living with a

JOHN ROEDEL

new passion

the shape of love
is a quiet hospital
be surrounded by
loudly singing angels

the shape of love
is a scratched up
wedding ring
resting on a
scratched up hand

the shape of love
is the feel of a
still pen between my
shaking fingers
and an untouched piece
of rustic paper

the shape of love
is a bedroom
with no clocks
where time moves

UNTIED

and tastes just like
maple syrup

the shape of love
is the way you
unknowingly sway
your hips along with
to the rhythms of
a summer rainstorm

the shape of love
is red pasta
red wine
red tablecloths
red lips
red curtains
red wax
red dresses
red skin
Red rain by Gabriel
&
red velvet cake

the shape of love

JOHN ROEDEL

is a friend
across the table
describing the
beauty you refuse to
see in yourself

the shape of love
is opening every
locked door that
you hide behind

the shape of love
is a gravestone
covered in dried
flowers

the shape of love
is both the valley
and the hilltop

the shape of love
is watching you
sleep

UNTIED

the shape of love
is a wildflower
coming up through
cobblestone

the shape of love
is how I write your
name on my arm
whenever I think
of you

the shape of love
are the embers you
leave in my hair
whenever I fall into
your gaze

the shape of love
is the coin we place
into the hands of a beggar

the shape of love
is a tree that we sit
under and allow

JOHN ROEDEL

it to give us a sermon
on blooming mercy

the shape of love
are the scars of
every victim that
are turned into
badges of courage

the shape of love
is a "do not disturb"
sign on a hotel door

the shape of love
is the word
"Gratitude"
written over
and over
and over
and over
and...

the shape of love
is the way you look

UNTIED

at me when we continue dance
long after the music has stopped

the shape of love
is a text from
just the right person
at just the right time

the shape of love
is how to taught me
that searching for beauty
is the only adventure
worth taking

the shape of love
has no official form

it's the smoke of your fire
it's the rainwater of your heartbreak
it's the nebula in your touch
&
it's the apparitions you leave on my tongue

love can look like everything

JOHN ROEDEL

and everything can look like love

love is neither organized or tidy

love is a brilliant mess
of stained carpets
broken windows
and open wounds

love isn't a museum
it has no bricks
or doors
or form

the shape of love is whatever
that's will hold you during
the long night

it's part cradle
part field
part spirit
part flesh
part song
part wave

UNTIED

part thread

yet all divine

it's a living breathing
muddle of
scent and sound
and sight and seduction
and service and sympathy
and soft embraces and striking thunder
and small mercies
and fierce words
and whispered promises
and rising purpose
and soft skin
and jagged laughter
and the space between us
and the way we get tangled up

and everything else in between

Didja?

Didja know that
the map to how we will rise again
was given to us right as we quickly fell
and didja know that
the water required to put out our fire
is usually hidden somewhere in our hell?

Didja know that
the deep ache we feel in our heart
is usually what keeps it awake to beat
and didja know that
the way to endure the terrible bitterness
is to remember that it's often followed by the sweet?

UNTIED

Didja know that
the night sky can grow the most jagged teeth
that chew ravenous on our ego while we sleep
and didja know that
the more we let our pride get eaten up
the more of ourselves that we get to keep?

Didja know that
the fact that our hands and knees are shaking
is evidence that we are both still alive
and didja know that
the tears that we allow to freely come
contain real proof that we will survive?

Didja know that
the things that cause us to feel pain
are always a very curious sort of creature
and didja know that
while they are always an unwelcome sight
they are also always the best sort of teacher

JOHN ROEDEL

Didja know that

suffering leads to growth and to new scars

suffering leads to hurt and to a world fully changed

and didja know that

to know peace you must often first know pain

it's this transaction of grace that I find most strange?

Pointing North

What I've never told you

about myself before is that

every time I hold a compass

my hands start to shake and then

I have to go lie down for a while.

Do you understand

what I'm talking about?

Let me explain:

I've been putting off

making the biggest decision

any of us can make.

UNTIED

Be a part?
Or
Stay apart?

There comes a moment in
all of our lives where we
must make the decision
whether we will be
a part of this world
or remain apart from it altogether

What will it be?

Are you going to take part
in the untamed sublime rumpus
of this world knowing that
well-meaning people inhabiting it
could turn you into debris?

Or

Will you choose to cautiously stay apart
from this swirling triple scoop disaster

JOHN ROEDEL

of charms and bloodletting
knowing that the long loneliness
can kill you a thousand times
before death ever comes to claim you.

What's your poison?

Will you take part?
Or be apart?

The crossroads is coming for all of us.

Bravely enter the heart grinder of this world
Or
Stay in bed so long that it swallows us whole?

Until now I've been undecided
on which path to take.

I've been hedging my bets.

I've tried to keep one foot
in the world
and one foot in my cave

UNTIED

Sometimes I tried and
take part in the adventure
and sometimes I couldn't be so brave.

I often plotted my course
without any worry and
I unfolded the great map

But then I would usually
put down my compass and
instead take a long nap

Half of me wanted to
be out there in the
ruckus with you all

and half of me wanted to
stay inside watching
the late day shadows crawl

I needed it both ways -
to be wildly connected to the world
while remaining wholly untouched by it

JOHN ROEDEL

The older that I got
I realized that we can't chase any
horizons from our couch

There is a vein of gold
for each of us out there
with our initials burned into it

It won't come to us
unless we open and strut
through the front door of our purpose

What will it be?

A part
Or
Apart?

Knots
or strings?

I've made my choice.
What about you?

UNTIED

Good.

Look for me.
I'll meet you out there.

I'll be the one holding a compass
with trembling hands.

Sky Born

birds fighting
the cutting wind

I'm fighting
my raging mind

we are in this
together

these little birds
and I

struggling to get
to our horizons

JOHN ROEDEL

against the winter gales
opposing us

The Brushstrokes in Your Eyes

Are you still awake?
I've told you all of this before
but

you are a piece of
celestial art

everything particle in you
has been softly kissed
by the lips of heaven

your eyelashes were
delicately sewn in
by angels with incandescent hands

UNTIED

the freckles on your back are a plotted
map of the universe that the divine
gave you to find your way back home

your heartbeats were handwritten
long ago by a poet who loved you
from the moment they first held a pen

every single shape and curve of you
was molded by the sculptor who
existed before eternity

you are proof of the master's touch

you are evidence of the great artist

you are a breathing Monet

you are a blessed relic of a gentle creator

you are the melody of an unseen composer

I know you see a mess

JOHN ROEDEL

when you look inside
the deep well in of your eyes

I know you see a murky pond of
unwept teardrops and
lost opportunity resting in still water

but that's not what I see

I see the pot ready to boil

I see the bubbles of your purpose

I see the coming steam

listen,
I see the brushstrokes in your eyes
of a thoughtful painter
who made you from the
same beauty that were used
to form watercolor nebulas

I see the same colors in your hair
that were given to the first sunset

UNTIED

I hear the same song on your tongue
that hummingbirds carry on their wings

I smell the same sacred clay on your skin
that potters use to craft masterpieces

I can taste the spring
on your reborn lips

It's all in you
I see it all
everybody does

You are a piece
of celestial art

I know I've told you all of this before
are you still awake?

JOHN ROEDEL

The Kindest of Jagged Pieces

words feel like red puzzle pieces
piling up in my mouth

when I part my lips so slight they just
all come spilling out

the words all clicking and snapping
together while floating in midair

giving sound to the madness and joy
inside of me that I can't solely bear

the space between us is a coffee table
where I'm arranging a picture of my heart

UNTIED

will I display something beautiful or terrifying?
will it be a brick wall or a work of art?

I wish that every time I build these invisible
word puzzles that I'd keep in mind

that of all the pieces I can offer the world
I need to choose the ones most kind

JOHN ROEDEL

Knots Into String

The shrewd fox is in the farmhouse
The therapy goat flies on a plane
The military monkey is playing roulette
I think that I might be going insane

The wind has a blade to it
The snow buried a coal train
The grass isn't growing out front
I have only your lips to blame

The moon became a blood martyr
The stars all joined a local gym
The aliens showed up in glitter
I have surrendered once again

UNTIED

The gemstones want a vote
The Lapis has a political beef
The Yellow Jade has seduced you
I will keep this eulogy brief

The fruit flies have all gathered
The beetles are under their skin
The roaches bought into a timeshare
I have plagiarized your original sin

The bus driver saw a miracle
The deacon met his match
The president became a crow
I have an itch that I can't scratch

The wildfires were a warning
The comet keeps getting the short straws
The zombies came early for breakfast
I have mental wellness in full pause

The Ted Talks are on repeat
The inspiration has all run dry
The robots now write poetry

JOHN ROEDEL

I am stuck on saying goodbye

The construction zone is spreading
The detours have become a maze
The foreman are drinking their lunch
I am sorry for all of my wasted days

The children are taking over
The inmates now run the east cell blocks
The authority lost their danger whistles
I'm off to visit more oceans than docks

The spring rolls straight into winter
The thaw has become the freeze
The snowmen all formed a union
I lived my life like an almost sneeze

The soup lines ran out of chicken broth
The CEO upstair just bought a pink fur coat
The Government withheld our paychecks
I only have as much value as what I last wrote

The moving vans are out front
The house has been foreclosed

UNTIED

The locks have been changed
I am naked and completely exposed

The sunlight is hiding behind Walgreens
The night is here to collect its fat debts
The midnight will likely last forever
I am leaving with zero to a hundred regrets

The singer is on her last verse
The poet can no longer rhyme
The pencil lost its sharp tip
I will become a spirit of time

The memories of us are in sepia
The pictures were hung for all to see
The feeling of our lands laced will linger
I need you to remember all of me

All of my so very good
And all of my so very grim
All of who I became later
And everything I've been

The afterlife is a phonebooth

JOHN ROEDEL

The operators all have wings
The lines are all now open
I left my knots behind for strings

About the Author:

John Roedel is a Wyoming based poet who is trying his best to chase miracles.

UNTIED

He published the popular book "Hey God. Hey John.: What Happens When God Writes Back." in the summer of 2018. It is the story about his complicated relationship with the divine.

This is John's second collection of poetry.

For more info on John please visit HeyGodHeyJohn.com